W9-BDH-620

THE STAR-SPANGLED GIRL

PUBLIC LIBRARY
STONEHAM, MASS.

The
STAR-
SPANGLED
GIRL

Neil Simon

RANDOM HOUSE · NEW YORK

812
Si5s

FIRST PRINTING

© Copyright, 1967, by Nancy Enterprises

All rights including the right of reproduction in whole or in part, in any form, are reserved under International and Pan-American Copyright Conventions. Published in New York by Random House, Inc., and simultaneously in Toronto, Canada Limited.

CAUTION: Professionals and amateurs are hereby warned that THE STAR-SPANGLED GIRL is fully protected under the Universal Copyright Convention, Berne Convention and Pan-American Copyright Convention and is subject to royalty. All rights are strictly reserved including professional, amateur, motion picture, television and radio recitation, lecturing, public reading and foreign language translation, and none of such rights can be exercised or used without written permission from the copyright owner. All inquiries for license and permissions should be addressed to: Albert DaSilva, 4 West 56th Street, New York, N.Y.

The amateur acting rights of THE STAR-SPANGLED GIRL are controlled exclusively by the Dramatists Play Service, Inc., 440 Park Avenue South, New York, New York 10016, without whose permission in writing no amateur performance of it may be made.

Photographs by courtesy of Sam Siegel

Library of Congress Catalog Card Number: 67-25079

MANUFACTURED IN THE UNITED STATES OF AMERICA

4.50 - 3.00   D9F

JUL 24 1968

THE STAR-SPANGLED GIRL *was first presented by Saint-Subber at the Plymouth Theatre, New York City, on December 21, 1966, with the following cast:*

(In order of appearance)

ANDY HOBART	Anthony Perkins
NORMAN CORNELL	Richard Benjamin
SOPHIE RAUSCHMEYER	Connie Stevens

Directed by George Axelrod
Scenic Production by Oliver Smith
Lighting by Jean Rosenthal
Costumes by Ann Roth

Synopsis of Scenes

The entire action of the play takes place in a duplex studio apartment in San Francisco.

Act One

Scene 1: It's late afternoon, in early summer.
Scene 2: Three days later.

Act Two

Scene 1: The next day, about 5 p.m.
Scene 2: A few days later.

Act Three

The next day. Early afternoon.

Act One

The curtains open on a duplex studio apartment over-looking the bay in San Francisco—it's not as nice as it sounds. It's a wood-shingled building about fifty years old. It was probably once the large Victorian home of a wealthy family, and in due course fell to its present state, an apartment and furnished-room multiple dwelling. Still, it's not without its charm.

The apartment is shared by two young men, ANDY HOBART *and* NORMAN CORNELL. *However, at first glance, one can see that their "home" has a double function. It also serves as their place of business, the offices of their small magazine* Fallout. *On the first level the entrance to the apartment is stage center, at the top of three stairs. Stage right center is a long kitchen bar.*

It's late afternoon, in early summer. The door opens and ANDY HOBART *enters. He is about twenty-six, but has the worried look of a man twice his age.* ANDY *is a dedicated, idealistic cynic charged with the energy of an angry generation. He wears an old tan sports jacket over his khaki trousers, a checked shirt and no tie. He carries a briefcase that has seen better days. As he enters, he looks over at the desk and seems amazed and annoyed not to see anyone sitting there.*

ANDY   Norman . . . ? You home? I take it by your silence that you're not home . . . (*He crosses to a tape recorder on the desk*) So where are you?
        (*He turns the machine on, and puts his briefcase down*)

3

NORMAN'S VOICE (*Offstage*) I'm up on the roof stealing
laundry . . . You may be wearing a pink housecoat tomorrow, but at least it'll be clean. How about those finished pages on the desk? (ANDY *picks them up and looks
through them*) I've been pounding the typewriter for
nine straight hours. I am now capable of committing the
perfect crime because I no longer have fingerprints . . .
Mr. Franklyn telephoned five times. I repeat, five times.
He said we owe him six hundred dollars in printing bills
and fifty cents for five telephone calls. He also said if he
doesn't get his money by Saturday, he's going to send
over his two sons to break our four legs. I told him I'm
just a writer and *you* take care of all bills, so they're going
to break your legs and just sprain my ankles. I am now
finished talking so please turn me off.
> (ANDY *turns off the tape recorder as the telephone
> rings. He answers it*)

ANDY *Fallout* magazine . . . Who's calling, please? Mr.
Franklyn? One moment, Mr. Franklyn, I'll give you our
billing department . . . (*He presses a button and uses a
Titus Moody voice. He sits on the pole table*) Billing
department . . . Yes . . . ? Oh, Mr. Franklyn. Yes, I
got your five messages . . . You mean you haven't re-
ceived our check . . . ? I can't understand that . . . Why
just yesterday . . . (*He presses down on the receiver and
cuts off the call. He looks over* NORMAN'S *pages. The
telephone rings again. He picks it up*) *Fallout* magazine . . . Oh, Mr. Franklyn. I guess you got cut off.
Sorry. I'll give you our billing department. (*He presses
the button and resumes a Titus Moody voice*) Billing
department . . . Oh, yes, Mr. Franklyn. Well—(*Again
he deliberately clicks off. He hangs up and waits. The
phone rings again.* ANDY *uses the nasal voice of a tele-*

phone operator) . . . And a fifty percent chance of showers today. Tomorrow morning, clearing with patches of fog—(*He winces as* FRANKLYN *hangs up hard*) I don't know what you're so sore about, Franklyn. You may not be getting your money, but at least you know it's going to rain. (*The telephone rings again.* ANDY *turns on the tape machine and records*) . . . Hey, Luigi, how about a little service? (*The telephone rings again and he records that too. He turns off the machine, picks up phone and takes it to the desk. Then, with an Italian accent, he answers it*) Luigi's Restaurant . . . Who? No, is no magazine. Is Luigi's Restaurant . . .

(*He turns on the tape and plays it back*)

ANDY'S VOICE   Hey, Luigi, how about a little service?

ANDY (*Still in Italian accent*)   Sí, sí, I'm-a coming. (*The phone's ringing is heard on the tape recorder*) 'Scusa, my other phone, she's-a ringing. (*He hangs up and rubs his hands with satisfaction*) I can keep this up as long as you can, Franklyn.

(*The roof door opens and* NORMAN *comes down the ladder carrying a basket of laundry.* NORMAN *is about the same age as* ANDY. *Although he is the brain, the intellect behind* Fallout, *when he is away from the typewriter he is an incorrigible adolescent*)

NORMAN (*On the balcony*)   I just saved us eight dollars in laundry bills. And I found you your blue shirt.

ANDY   I didn't lose one.

NORMAN   I didn't say you did. I just said I found you one.

ANDY   Did you have lunch today?

NORMAN (*Comes down the steps to the landing*)   Certainly. I had one sardine on a frozen waffle.

ANDY   Why?

NORMAN   Because that's all there was.

ANDY   You mean there's nothing else to eat in the refrigerator?

NORMAN   There's three ice cubes and a light bulb. I'm saving them for tomorrow. (*At the center table, he puts the basket down. Then he holds up a shirt*) I'll put this in the freezer. We don't have any more starch.
(*He takes the shirt into the kitchen*)

ANDY (*Sitting on the pole table*)   Norman, it's just occurred to me that being poor is very boring. We really wouldn't have to worry about money if you would let me do what I suggested.

NORMAN (*Comes out of the kitchen and goes down right to the table between the sofas*)   What was that?

ANDY   Selling you to a medical school.

NORMAN   Never mind me, how about selling the magazine? How'd you do today?

ANDY   If selling two subscriptions is good, we only did fair. (NORMAN *picks up an empty box of cookies*) Somehow I don't think the average San Francisco housewife is ready for a politically controversial magazine that is definitely anti-American . . . Is there any mail?

NORMAN (*Throws down the empty box*) In the waste-basket. (*He walks to the center table*) I'm so hungry. (*He puts the clothesbasket on the floor, downstage of the left chair. Then he eats crumbs from a plate on the table*)

ANDY (*He picks up the wastebasket, puts it on the pole table and goes through the bills*) Printing bills, type-writer repair bills, rent bills, electric bills, food bills, gas bills. This is a bill for the waste paper basket.

NORMAN (*Running his finger around the empty jam jar in search of food*) And we owe the lady from the pet shop eighty cents.

ANDY The pet shop? What for?

NORMAN She gave me a haircut today.

ANDY (*He returns the wastebasket to left of desk*) Let me worry about the bills, Norman, you write the maga-zine. I need your blue jacket. I've got to go out tonight. (*He goes up left and gets the blue jacket hanging upstage of a bulletin board*)

NORMAN Business?

ANDY Why else would I do the Monkey until three o'clock in the morning at the Velvet Cucumber?

NORMAN Who are you going with?

ANDY   Who do I go with every night? Our landlady, Mrs.
Mackininee. (*He takes the jacket to the sofa, where he
lifts up the top mattress and lays the jacket between the
mattress and springs. He drops the mattress down.* NOR-
MAN *looks for food in the drawers of the slant-top desk*)
Norman, you have no idea what I go through to keep us
from being thrown out on the street. (ANDY *kneels on
top of the mattress—he puts all his weight on it—to press
the suit*) Not only is she totally lacking in rhythm, but
she has no sense of direction. Last night she Watusied out
the door and into the parking lot.

> (*He rises and gets a dumbbell. Then rolls it over the
> mattress*)

NORMAN   (*Good-naturedly, at slant-top desk eating from a
small cereal box he has found*)   It'll go down as one of
the great sacrifices in journalistic history.

ANDY   You don't think it's humiliating to sit in a night
club with a dark-haired widow who wears blonde braids
and picks up the bill?

NORMAN   She likes you, doesn't she? Why don't you take
her to the beach for the weekend so we can have the
apartment painted?

> (*He sits at the desk*)

ANDY   You think I want to fall off her motorcycle the way
her husband did?

NORMAN   Listen, anytime you want to change places I'm
perfectly willing.

> (*The telephone rings.* NORMAN *gets up hurriedly
> and motions to* ANDY *to answer it as he goes to the*

chair left of the center table. He then sits and begins to fold clean socks. ANDY *crosses left, above the table, to answer the phone)*

ANDY (*Into phone, Titus Moody voice again*) Billing department . . . ! (*Changes to his normal voice*) Oh, Mrs. Mackininee . . . No, no, I wasn't trying to sound older. I think I caught a cold last night. Yes, on the back of the motorcycle . . . You really are a wonderful driver . . . Did you ever find your other braid? Oh, too bad. I feel kind of responsible . . . Well, I do—I mean I felt myself slipping off and it was the first thing I grabbed . . . Yes, I'll pick you up at eight o'clock . . . Oh, that sounds wonderful. I can't wait to see them. 'Bye.

NORMAN You can't wait to see what?

ANDY Her new gold-sequined goggles. You can imagine how they look with her silver-lamé jumpsuit . . . Promise me one thing.

NORMAN What?

ANDY If there's a crash and they find my body next to hers, tell my mother and father I was kidnapped.
(ANDY *goes and pulls the suit from under the sofa and walks to the stairs with it*)

NORMAN Listen, when you come home tonight, I want to hear everything that happened. I don't care what time it is, wake me up and tell me.

ANDY All right, Norman.

9

NORMAN   Don't say all right. Promise me. You'll wake me up and you'll tell me everything. Don't leave anything out.

ANDY (*Leans over the balcony. He looks at* NORMAN *with concern*)   Norman, I think you've been working too hard lately. Why don't you take the night off and go see a sexy movie?

NORMAN   How can I take the night off? We've got a magazine to get out here.

ANDY   You've got five days to finish three articles. You can do that with two fingers. Why don't you call up a girl?

NORMAN   You can't just call up a girl. You have to know her first.

ANDY   Well, call up a girl you know.

NORMAN   I don't like any of the girls I know. I only like the girls *you* know.

ANDY   All right, call up one of my girls.

NORMAN   I can't. I don't know them.
(NORMAN *rises and takes the clothesbasket into the kitchen. He returns and goes to the desk*)

ANDY   Norman, I'm as dedicated to this magazine as you are. Maybe even more. You put your talent into it; I put in my blood. And it's my job to preserve that talent and keep it in perfect working order. That's why I want you to relax once in a while. If you don't, you're going to get a bubble on your head.

NORMAN (*Seated at the desk*)   I'll go out as soon as this issue is finished.

ANDY   Who will you go out with?

NORMAN   A beautiful, gorgeous blonde will move into the empty apartment next door and I'll fall madly in love. All right?

ANDY   All right, Norman, if you're happier working, then I'm happy. Work all night and enjoy yourself.
(*He goes into the room and closes the door.* NORMAN *sits at the typewriter and picks up the clippings. He talks aloud to himself*)

NORMAN   I don't know how he expects me to finish a magazine if I don't sit down and finish it . . . Things do not get written by themselves—unless he believes in elves and gnomes . . . And they don't write magazines, they repair shoes . . .
(*He begins to type. The doorbell rings. He gets up, crosses to the door and opens it.* SOPHIE RAUSCH-MEYER, *a lovely young blonde, stands there. She is everything* NORMAN *has described. She is the prototype of the all-American girl. If she had a few freckles on her nose it would be perfect. Her compact, solid form and freshly scrubbed face tell us that this is a purely physical creature. What she can't do with an intellectual problem, she more than makes up for with her strong backstroke or her straight back when astride a horse. The Arkansas*

*drawl doesn't add to her image as an intellect either.
And best of all, she smells good)*

SOPHIE *(With a big, warm smile)* Excuse me. Mah name
is Sophie Rauschmeyer. Ah just moved into the empty
apartment next door. Ah know people in big cities don't
usually do this, but Ah promised mah folks Ah would
make mah akwaitance with mah neighbors so Ah just
want to say it's a pleasure meetin' you and hope Ah see
you again. Real soon. 'Bye!
*(She gives him a big smile. She turns, closes the
door and goes. NORMAN has not flinched a muscle
since she appeared. He now seems to be frozen to
the spot and stands motionless for what seems to be
an hour and a half)*

ANDY *(Comes out of his room, wearing the blue jacket, no
shoes)* Did someone just ring the bell . . . ? Norman,
did someone just come in?
(He leans down and taps NORMAN on his head)

NORMAN What? What? *(Quickly)* No! No! No one came
in. There's no one here. Go back to your room.

ANDY What's the matter, Norman?

NORMAN There's nothing the matter. Leave me alone. Go
back to your room. Can't you see I'm busy working.

ANDY At the door?

NORMAN I needed some air.

ANDY Why don't you open the window?

NORMAN I don't want fresh air. I want plain air . . . will you please go back to your room?

ANDY All right, Norman. Don't tense up. Relax. Try and relax. (*He is about to go back into his room when the doorbell rings again.* ANDY *stops and looks at* NORMAN, *who doesn't move*) Now I hear a bell.

NORMAN All right, so you hear a bell. People ring bells all day long. It's no reason for you to loiter on top of the stairs all night.
(*The doorbell rings again*)

ANDY Are you going to answer that or am I?

NORMAN *I'm* going to answer it. Stay up there.
(*He looks at* ANDY, *hoping he'll go away. But he knows he won't so* NORMAN *opens the door.* SOPHIE *stands there again. She has a cake in her hands*)

SOPHIE (*Big smile again*) Excuse me again . . . Ah was just unpackin' and mah friends back home sent me this fruit cake with rum in it which Ah'm not allowed to eat 'cause Ah'm in trainin', and Ah'd hate to see it go to waste so Ah'd appreciate it if you'd accept it with mah compliments. (*She gives him the cake*) Nice seein' you again. 'Bye.
(*She pulls the door shut and exits.* NORMAN *gives a long look at the door*)

ANDY Who's that, Norman?

NORMAN Never mind who it is, I saw her first.

13

ANDY   All right, you saw her first. Who is she?

NORMAN (*Turns front*)   Her name is Sophie Rauschmeyer and she just moved into the empty apartment next door and she just gave me a fruit cake with rum in it and I love her. (*Running left, right, and all over the room*) Wahoo! Did you see what moved into this building? Next door to where I live! (*He puts the cake on the pole table*) It's for me. All for me. God loves me and He gave me something wonderful.
(*He stands with arms outstretched*)

ANDY (*Happy for* NORMAN, *on the bottom step*)   I was going to get you one for Christmas.

NORMAN (*He is now dancing all over the room*)   Did you smell her? Did you get one whiff of that fragrance? Did you open your entire nose and smell that girl?

ANDY (*Comes down onto the stage floor and goes stage left*)   I was upstairs, she didn't smell that far . . . I need your dancing shoes.
(ANDY *picks up the cake, gives it to* NORMAN, *and then pushes him onto the pole table*)

NORMAN   Didn't smell that far? It's all over the room. (ANDY *pulls the director's chair left, sits down and starts pulling off* NORMAN's *shoes*) It's even out in the hall. I'll bet she's inundated the whole lousy neighborhood. They're gonna start raising rents. And you stay away from her.

ANDY   No contest. She's not my type.

NORMAN Well, she's my type. (*He takes the cake to the kitchen—in stocking feet*) How do you know what type she is?

ANDY (*He pulls the chair back to the center table and gets the rubber stamp*) Norman, when it comes to girls, I have extrasensory perception. (*He applies the stamp to the pad, then to the shoes*) She's the all-outdoor type. Enormously strong from the neck down.

NORMAN (*He returns from the kitchen, and goes to the right of the center table*) Who cares what her I.Q. is? I'm not giving out any Fulbrights. I just want to smell her and touch her.

ANDY All right. Go ring her doorbell and say you want to smell her and touch her.

NORMAN Are you crazy, didn't you hear the way she talked? "Ah'm glad to make yo' akwaitance"—she comes from Rhett Butler country. The only way to make it with a girl like that is with romance, big gestures.

ANDY All right. Go out and burn down Atlanta. She'll be crazy about you.

NORMAN (*Going left, downstage of the table*) You think I wouldn't do it if I could get to nibble on her chin for an hour?

ANDY I was right. You've been working much too hard lately.
       (*He rises and goes right to the stairs*)

NORMAN (*Follows* ANDY) Wait a minute. Talk to me. (ANDY *stops on the stairs and gets the tie hanging on the landing balustrade*) Help me. I've got to plan this all very carefully. I mustn't jump into anything. One wrong move and I can blow the entire love affair . . . Flowers? What about flowers? Flowers every morning. Flowers twice a day . . . No. No. That's not big enough.

ANDY (*Still on the stairs, he puts on the tie*) How about trees?

NORMAN Maybe it shouldn't be big. Maybe it should be small. Something with thought. Something personal. What could I do for her that's very small and very personal?

ANDY How about brushing her teeth?

NORMAN Get outa here! You're killing everything. You have no idea how to treat a girl like that.

ANDY Personally I wouldn't try, but if she excites your nasal passages, Norman, I'm with you.

NORMAN I got it! I got it! Where's the paint can? I need a can of green paint.
    (*He goes stage left and gets the paint can from under the table*)

ANDY What are you going to do?

NORMAN (*Goes to* ANDY) I'm going to paint the stairs. One letter on each step. So that when she comes home at night and goes up the stairs, it's going to read (*He indi-*

cates with his finger pointing up the stairs) . . . I-love-you-Sophie-Rauschmeyer.

ANDY But she's already upstairs. When she goes down in the morning it's going to say Reymshaur-Ephos-Ouvlie!

NORMAN (*Goes down right*) Why do I bother talking to you?

ANDY I'm going to meet Mrs. Mackininee. (*Crosses to the door*) If I'm still alive, I'll be back at two A.M. . . . If not, about three-thirty.
  (*He exits. Blackout*)

*The lights come up. It is three days later. The room is
empty. The door opens and* ANDY *enters carrying his briefcase, having just returned from another grueling afternoon
of selling.*

ANDY   Hi, Norman, how's it going? (*He stops and looks
at the desk, but* NORMAN *isn't there. He walks into the
room—he looks upset. He puts down his briefcase upstage of the radiator and crosses to the tape recorder*)
All right, Norman, where the hell are you? (*The telephone rings.* ANDY *doesn't answer it. It rings again. He
pushes the receiver into the waste paper basket. Then he
picks it up*) Hello . . . ? Oh, Mr. Franklyn . . . I'm
sorry I didn't answer the phone sooner, but I couldn't
find it. I still have the bandages on my eyes—oh, didn't
I tell you? Well, the doctor says my only chance is to
have the operation. The only trouble is, it's six hundred
dollars . . . Yes, the same amount I owe you . . . But
I'm determined to pay your bill rather than have the
operation—unless you have another suggestion . . . You
like the first one best . . .
      (*We hear a pounding on the front door*)

NORMAN'S VOICE (*Offstage*)   Andy, hurry up. Open the
door. I forgot my key.
      (ANDY *crosses to the door and opens it.* NORMAN
      rushes in with a large package of groceries)

ANDY   Where've you been all day?

NORMAN (*Taking the groceries to the center table*) In love. Don't talk to me now. I'm busy.
(*He crosses to the desk, takes off his jacket, and puts it on the desk-chair*)

ANDY I know you've been busy, but you haven't been working. I just looked on the desk; there are no new pages.

NORMAN (*Goes upstairs to his room for a fancy basket*) I've got plenty of time. Plenty of time.

ANDY Not anymore we don't. We have three days. Three days to finish three articles.

NORMAN I'm thinking all the time. I've got everything up here.
(*He points to his head and starts downstairs*)

ANDY One! Give me one article. Give me one title you've thought of since the day that Arkansas frangipani checked in here and you painted love letters up and down the staircase . . . Let's hear one title!

NORMAN "The Real Case Against Fluoridation. Is Tooth Cancer Next?"

ANDY Write it. Sit down and write it. Now!

NORMAN Don't coerce me. I can't work under coercion.

ANDY How about under savage beating? I got a life savings and three years of work tied up in this venture. And I'm not going to see something good and vital and worthwhile go down the drain because you can't think of anything else but that corn-fed Minnie Mouse next door. What's in that package?

NORMAN   Groceries.

ANDY   I buy the groceries. It's for her, isn't it? What have you got in there?

NORMAN (*Indignantly picks up the bag*)   None of your business. It's private groceries.

ANDY (*Looks at the package which* NORMAN *is holding*) The United Nations Gourmet Shoppe?

NORMAN   They always have a big sale before Lent.

ANDY (*Snaps his fingers and points to the table.* NORMAN *obeys and puts the bag down.* ANDY *starts to take out some of the cans and jars and examines them*)   Miniature watermelon . . . ? Baby Siberian herring filets . . . ? Tiny kumquats . . . ? Who's coming for dinner, a couple of midgets?

NORMAN   I had a yen for some delicacies.
        (*He goes left, below the table, to the desk*)

ANDY   Delicacies? You haven't eaten anything fancier than a banana and peanut-butter sandwich since the day I met you. (*Puts the jars back. He reaches in the bag and takes out the bill—he is shocked*) Twenty-two dollars?? You spent twenty-two dollars for *toy food*?

NORMAN   Take it out of my share of the profits.

ANDY Your share of the profits can't pay for your banana and peanut-butter sandwiches. Are you out of your mind?

NORMAN I'm giving her a gift. You gave your mother a gift on Mother's Day, didn't you?

ANDY I gave her a year's subscription to our magazine. You hardly even know this girl.

NORMAN I know her. (*Goes to the telescope.* ANDY *crosses to the desk for glue and dummy magazine*) I know she works like a dog six days a week. I watch her through the telescope running after that bus every morning. I watch her coming home every night. Tired. Hungry. (*Goes left to* ANDY) That sweet, beautiful girl coming home to nothing better for dinner than a can of Broadcast Corned Beef Hash.

ANDY How do you know that?

NORMAN I check her garbage every afternoon.

ANDY All right, Norman, get a hold of yourself.
(*He sits on the pole table*)

NORMAN Get a hold of myself? Are you kidding? My functioning days are over. I've become an animal. I've developed senses no man has ever used before. I can smell the shampoo in her hair three city blocks away. I can have my radio turned up full blast and still hear her taking off her stockings! Don't you understand, SHE TURNS ME ON! From my head to my toes, I take one look at her and I light up. This month alone my personal electric bill will be over two hundred dollars . . .
(*He starts putting the jars and cans into the basket*)

ANDY (*Glues a clipping onto the page of the dummy magazine*) You know, when I first met you in high school, I thought you were eccentric. When we worked on the journal together in college, I thought you were a very promising fruit cake. The last couple of years I decided you were a tremendously talented bedbug. Now I know what you are . . . (*He rises, and goes a few steps right*) *You are the unhatched egg of an illiterate looney bird!* We've got three days to get out a magazine and you spend your time buying pygmy cucumbers for a girl with strong shampoo?

NORMAN I'm going to let that pass. I am also not going to waste time trying to explain something that cannot be explained. Because it would be a waste of time.

ANDY You've already cornered the waste of time market. Explain it to me.

NORMAN Did you ever hear of physical attraction? Pure, unadulterated physical attraction?

ANDY I have.

NORMAN What is it?

ANDY It's when one hippopotamus likes another hippopotamus with no questions asked.

NORMAN Exactly. Now it's five-thirty and my hippopotamus will be getting off her bus. Now leave me alone because I've got work to do.
(*He takes the cans and jars out of the bag and puts them on the table*)

ANDY   All right . . . Look, I'll put the kumquats in the basket and you finish the article.

NORMAN   Who are you, Miles Standish? I'll put my own kumquats in the basket. (*He goes left, upstage of* ANDY) A ribbon! I need a red ribbon. You got a red ribbon?

ANDY   Do I have a red ribbon?

NORMAN   Either you have a red ribbon or you don't. If you have a red ribbon, I'd like it for my basket, please.

ANDY   I'm not going to discuss red ribbons with you at this time.

NORMAN   In other words, you're not going to give me your red ribbon!

ANDY   That's right. Out of the *thousands* I have saved in my closet, I'm not going to give you a red ribbon.

NORMAN   (*He goes up the stairs to the landing*)   That's one I owe you, Andy. From now on I'm keeping score. (*He glances out the window*) There's her bus. (*He looks through the telescope*) I almost missed her bus account of you.

ANDY   Get away from that window.

NORMAN   Are you crazy? And miss Sophie getting off the bus? You know I wait for this all day.
     (*He looks through the telescope, focusing it*)

ANDY   (*He takes a few steps right*)   Norman, write me two

23

more articles and I'll buy you a bigger telescope. You'll be able to zoom right into her shoes. What do you say?

NORMAN (*Looking through the telescope*) I could have missed her bus. Sophie is on that bus and I almost missed it.

ANDY (*He crosses up the stairs to the window and puts his hand over the lens, covering it*) Damn you, Norman, answer me!

NORMAN (*Still looking through the telescope. He screams*) Oh, my God! Sophie! (*He looks up and sees that* ANDY *has his hand covering the opening*) You idiot! I thought her bus fell into a hole. Get your hand off my lens opening!

ANDY My hand stays on your opening until you make me a promise.

NORMAN I promise! I promise! Now get out of the way. (ANDY *comes down the stairs*) *There she is!* Oh, Mother in Heaven, will you look at that girl! Look at her! Just look at that girl!

ANDY All right, let me see.

NORMAN (*Screams*) Stay away from here. (ANDY *hangs up his jacket on the bulletin-board hook, then sits on the pole table*) I'm looking at her. Oh, you wonderful crazy Sophie. She has got without a doubt the most magnificent earlobes on the face of the earth. (*He looks out the window, straight down*) She's in the building. She'll be upstairs any minute. (*He runs down the steps, picks up the*

basket from the table and goes to the desk) You're not
going to give me your red ribbon, right?

ANDY Who do you think I am, Fanny Farmer?

NORMAN That's two I owe you.
(*He sits at the typewriter, puts the basket on the
floor and rips the paper out of the machine. Then he
puts in another piece and begins to type*)

ANDY What are you doing? Are you working . . . ? Norman, sweetheart, what are you writing? (*Rises and goes
to peer over his shoulder. He then reads aloud*) . . .
Adomis terra amorta eternos . . . What is that, a pre-
scription?

NORMAN It's "I worship the ground you walk on" in Latin.
It goes with the groceries. (*He rises and puts the note
in the basket, then faces* ANDY) Now get out of my way
or you get Alberta peaches in brandy right between the
eyes.
(ANDY *moves and* NORMAN *starts to the door as the
telephone rings*)

ANDY (*Calls after* NORMAN) Norman, you've got three
minutes to deliver your Care package. (*Picks up the
phone*) United Nations Gourmet Shoppe . . . Oh,
hello, Mrs. Mackininee, how are you . . . ? The beach
this weekend? Gee, I don't know. I've developed this aw-
ful cough . . . Yes, I'm disappointed too.

NORMAN (*Rushes in*) She's got it! She's got the basket!
(*He runs back to the door*)

25

ANDY (*Into the phone*) Yes, I agree it would be a lot more fun than staying home and collecting rents. What time do you want to go?

NORMAN (*Holding the door open and peeking through the crack*) She's reading the note.

ANDY (*Into the phone*) How?

NORMAN She's moving her gorgeous lips and reading the note.

ANDY (*Into the phone*) You mean I hold onto you and the surfboard at the same time? Won't that be a problem going through tunnels?

NORMAN She's looking over here . . . Here she comes! (*Closes the door and runs screaming to the center table*) Clean the apartment! Hurry up! (*He takes the grocery bag to upstage of bar*) Clean the apartment! (ANDY *hangs up the phone*) I'm shaking. (*Rushes left to* ANDY) Look at that hand shaking. Andy, I'm scared to death.

ANDY *You're* scared? I'm going surfing tomorrow with a daredevil landlady. They'll find me washed up in Hawaii.
(*The doorbell rings*)

NORMAN Open the door! Open the door! (*The doorbell rings again.* ANDY *turns to go*) Where are you going?

ANDY To open the door.

NORMAN Don't open the door. I'm not ready yet. (NORMAN *puts his jacket around his shoulders and gets a pipe*

26

*from the slant-top desk, which he puts in his mouth—
upside down. Then he sits above the desk and poses)*
Open it! Open it!

    (ANDY *opens the door and* SOPHIE *enters carrying the
basket. She seems quite upset)*

SOPHIE (*To* ANDY)   Excuse me. (*To* NORMAN) Mr. Cornell, Ah have tried to be neighborly, Ah have tried to be
friendly and Ah have tried to be cordial . . . Ah don't
know what it is that you're tryin' to be. That first night
Ah was appreciative that you carried mah trunk up the
stairs . . . The fact that it slipped and fell five flights
and smashed to pieces was not your fault . . . Ah didn't
even mind that personal message you painted on the
stairs. Ah thought it was crazy, but sorta sweet. However, things have now gone too far . . . (*Goes down to
the pole table*) Ah cannot accept gifts from a man Ah
hardly know . . . (*Puts the basket on the pole table*)
Especially canned goods. And Ah read your little note.
Ah can guess the gist of it even though Ah don't speak
Italian. (ANDY *sits on the stool below the kitchen bar*)
This has got to stop, Mr. Cornell. Ah can do very well
without you leavin' little chocolate-almond Hershey bars
in mah mailbox—they melted yesterday, and now Ah got
three gooey letters from home with nuts in 'em—and Ah
can do without you sneakin' into mah room after Ah go
to work and paintin' mah balcony without tellin' me
about it. Ah stepped out there yesterday and mah slippers
are still glued to the floor. And Ah can do without you
tying big bottles of eau de cologne to mah cat's tail. The
poor thing kept swishin' it yesterday and nearly beat herself to death . . . And most of all, Ah can certainly do
without you watchin' me get on the bus every day
through that high-powered telescope. You got me so

nervous the other day Ah got on the wrong bus. In short, Mr. Cornell, and Ah don't want to have to say this again, *leave me ay-lone!*
(*She turns and starts to go*)

NORMAN   Aside from that, is there any chance of your falling in love with me?
(SOPHIE *turns*)

SOPHIE   You are crackers, you know that, don't you? (*To* ANDY) Did you know your roommate is crackers?
(ANDY *crosses down right*)

ANDY   Yes, but I didn't know the exact medical term.

SOPHIE (*To* NORMAN)   Didn't you listen to one solitary word Ah said to you?

NORMAN   Yes, I'm listening . . . (*The jacket comes off his shoulders as he rises and goes above the pole table to* SOPHIE) I'm listening, I'm looking, and I'm smelling.
(*He sniffs*)

SOPHIE (*Yells and backs right*)   Ah don't want to be smelled! (NORMAN *follows and sniffs again. She moves right. To* ANDY) Tell him to stop smelling me.

ANDY (*Quietly*)   Norman, stop smelling her.
(*He sits on the sofa*)

SOPHIE (*To* NORMAN)   Ah am going to repeat this to you once more and for the last time. Ah am ingaged to be married to First Lieutenant Burt Fenneman of the United States Marine Corps. (*To* ANDY) And in six weeks Ah will be *Mrs.* First Lieutenant Burt Fenneman of the

United States Marine Corps. (*To* NORMAN) And Ah intend to be happily married to him for the rest of mah natural life. (*She takes a step left*) Do you understand that?

NORMAN (*Goes right to her*) Please lower your voice. I'm trying to hear your hair growing.

SOPHIE (*Goes right to* ANDY) What is wrong with him? Does he have oral trouble?

ANDY Oral trouble?

SOPHIE (*Points to her ears*) With his ears. Hard of hearing.

ANDY Yes, he has very bad orals.

SOPHIE Ah thought as much. (*Goes back to* NORMAN) Ah could have you arrested, you know that? For loiterin', breakin' 'n' enterin', tamperin' with mah mailbox, pesterin', peepin' tom'n'! Don't think Ah won't do it. (*She starts toward the door*)

NORMAN (*Stops her*) Then I'll have *you* arrested. For creamy smooth skin, perfect teeth, a ridiculously small nose, insanely gorgeous earlobes and an indecently fantastic, unbelievable fragrance.
(*He inhales*)

SOPHIE (*Screams*) Ah told you to stop smelling me! (*To* ANDY) Do something!

ANDY Do you want me to hold his nose?

NORMAN (*Moves right to her*) I'm sorry. A girl who looks like you shouldn't be allowed to walk the streets. (*Grabs her downstage arm*) This is a citizen's arrest!
> (*He starts pulling her with him toward the steps*)

SOPHIE (*She pulls away. To* ANDY) If he doesn't keep away from me, Ah'm going to arrange to have mah fiancé inflict bodily harm to him. Tell him that.

ANDY Norman, her fiancé is going to inflict your body with harm.

NORMAN Do you think that would stop me? Beatings? Flailings? Whippings? I welcome them. Tell her!

ANDY (*To* SOPHIE) He says he welcomes beatings, flailings and whippings.

SOPHIE Ah heard him!

ANDY She heard you.

NORMAN (*On the stairs*) If having a friend of yours punch me very hard is going to make you happy, my entire face is at your disposal.

SOPHIE Hey . . . Are we on one of those television programs or somethin'? If we are, Ah'd like to know. Otherwise Ah'm callin' Camp Pendleton.

ANDY Don't look at me. I'm just an innocent bystander.

SOPHIE So am I. Two years ago in Japan Ah represented mah country in the Olympic swimming competition. In order to be a member of the official United States Olympic swimming team, you must be in one hundred percent perfect physical condition. That's me. Ah was one hundred percent physically perfect. *Until* Ah moved next door. From the day Ah found that trail of little heart-shaped peanut brittles leading from mah door to his door, Ah have been a nervous wreck . . . Not only is it difficult to keep up with mah swimming, but Ah'm afraid to take a bath. Ah have found that when Ah brush mah hair, mah hair falls out. And the ones that fall out have not been replaced by new ones . . . Ah am twenty-three years old and that man is starting me on the road to total baldness. Ah intend to get married while Ah still have a full head of hair left. (*She goes to the door*) Ah am now going to have a dinner of good, basic American food, clean mah apartment and get ten hours' sleep. If Ah see him sittin' in that big tree outside mah window again, strummin' that ukelele and singin' those Spanish love songs, Ah'm gonna call for the United States Marines.

> (*She exits and slams the door.* NORMAN *and* ANDY *stand there for a brief second in silence. Then a wild gleam of uncontrolled happiness flashes across* NORMAN's *face*)

NORMAN (*Goes to the kitchen*) I'm getting to her, Andy . . . I tell you, I'm getting to her.

ANDY The only thing you're going to get is bayonet prac-tice . . . She's engaged, Norman, forget about her.

NORMAN (*Coming out of the kitchen*) Forget about her? Did you see what was just in this room? Did you see?

31

ANDY   I saw. It was a girl.

NORMAN (*Shocked. Comes down right to* ANDY)   A *girl?*
You call that a girl?? That's not a girl. *That* was one
of God's creations made during His *best* period! Don't
ever call her a girl in front of me again.
   (*He storms back into the kitchen*)

ANDY   Well, whatever that thing is, if it goes bald, you're
in big trouble with our armed forces.

NORMAN (*Comes out of the kitchen with a mop*)   I can
handle Uncle Sam.

ANDY   Where are you going with that?

NORMAN (*Crossing down left, he empties wastebasket on
the floor*)   You think I'm going to let her clean her apartment after she's been working all day?

ANDY (*Rises and goes to the bar. He gets the ukelele, and
goes stage left menacingly*)   All right, I've had just about
as much of King Kong and Fay Wray as I can take . . .
You move two steps away from that typewriter and for
the rest of this week you'll be picking ukelele out of
your head.

NORMAN   Not unless you're capable of swallowing an entire mop.

ANDY   Norman, what's happened to you? I've seen you
panting over a girl before, but this is the first time I
ever saw steam coming out of your ears . . . I'm worried
about you.

NORMAN   Don't you think I am too? I am definitely worried about me. I was up all last night rereading Krafft-Ebbing. In 1926 there was a case very similar to mine in Gutenburg, Germany. It involved a nun and a knockwurst salesman. (*He crosses to the door with the wastebasket and mop.* ANDY *then goes left, and leaves the ukelele on up left table*) But I can't help myself because I'm crazy about that girl. I'll do anything, including mopping her kitchen floor, to be with her every night for the rest of my life.

ANDY   In six weeks she's marrying the Marine.

NORMAN   What she does during the day is her business.
        (*He exits. The telephone rings.* ANDY *turns the tape recorder on to "record," and talks into the mike*)

ANDY (*In Chinese*)   Oh sing mah toh wan po soo chow moo ling. (*He turns the machine off. The telephone rings again. He quickly reruns the tape, then picks up the phone and speaks in his Chinese dialect*) Yes, please? Wo Ping's Chinese Gardens.
        (*He turns the machine on and we hear his voice from before*)

ANDY'S VOICE   Hey, Luigi, how about a little service?
        (*He quickly hangs up, and turns off the machine. The door flies open and* SOPHIE *storms in angrily*)

SOPHIE (*Shouts*)   Do you know what he's doing? Do you know what he's doing now?

ANDY   He's mopping your kitchen floor.

33

SOPHIE *He is mopping mah kitchen floor!*

ANDY And you don't want your kitchen floor mopped.

SOPHIE (*Screams*) Ah don't want it mopped 'cause Ah waxed it last night and now *he's moppin' up all the wax!*

ANDY I can hear you. I have perfect orals.

SOPHIE Don't you understand? He has illegally entered mah apartment and criminally mopped mah floor. Aren't you going to do anything except stand there?

ANDY If you'll calm down, maybe we can discuss this?

SOPHIE Of course. (*Crosses to the desk*) Ah just have to make one call. May Ah use your phone?

ANDY Certainly.

SOPHIE (*Dials once*) Thank you. Ah don't have one of mah own. (*Into the phone*) Hello? San Francisco Police.
     (ANDY *closes the door*)

ANDY You wouldn't.

SOPHIE Wouldn't I? (*Into the phone*) Ah'd like to report a demented man who's run amuck in mah kitchen.

ANDY (*Goes to* SOPHIE) Will you just listen to me for two minutes?

SOPHIE (*To* ANDY) In two minutes he will have mah

34

wallpaper steamed off and sent out to be dry cleaned. (*Into the phone*) That's right, run amuck . . . No, not with a knife, with a mop.

ANDY (*He tries to restrain her by holding her shoulder*) Give me sixty seconds.

SOPHIE   Take your hands off mah "ingaged" shoulder.

ANDY   Give me that phone.
(*He takes it from her*)

SOPHIE   It's just gonna cost you another dime 'cause Ah'm gonna call them again.

ANDY   Why won't you listen to me?

SOPHIE   Why? Ah'll tell you why. (*She crosses and picks up a lamp. She crosses back to him and turns the lamp on, holding it up to her cheek right in front of his face.* ANDY *puts phone on desk*) Look at mah skin. Those big, ugly red blotches are hives. Do you know what causes me to get hives?

ANDY   Holding a lamp to your face?

SOPHIE   Nervous tension causes me to get hives. And having mah floor mopped causes nervous tension. Ah am breaking out in big red blotches and Ah am losing mah hair and Ah have a date (*Puts the lamp back on the desk*) with mah fiancé tomorrow night and Ah'm going to look like a little old man with the measles . . . And you have the ultimate gall to ask me for time.
(*She goes right—upstage of* ANDY)

ANDY   I know exactly what you're going through. I've lived with that nut for three years and he's turned my hair grey.

SOPHIE (*Comes back downstage*)   Ah fail to notice it.

ANDY (*Goes to* SOPHIE)   Look at my eyelashes. All grey. I used to have long, beautiful black eyelashes. Did you ever see anything like that before? Grey! Grey! Grey!

SOPHIE (*Moves in close and scrutinizes*)   Grey eyelashes are not as noticeable on a man as a receding hairline is on a girl.
   (*She goes downstage*)

ANDY (*Being solicitous*)   It's not receding. You have beautiful hair.

SOPHIE   Do you like it?

ANDY   Very much.

SOPHIE   I'm glad. Because a lot of it has fallen on your floor. And if he's not out of there in five seconds, a lot of his blood is going to be on mah floor . . . Ah'm gonna start counting before Ah call again.

ANDY   No, you're not. You're going to sit down and listen to me.
   (*He gives her a gentle push toward a chair*)

SOPHIE (*Rises immediately*)   If you're threatening me Ah'd advise you not to. You're tall and skinny and Ah'm short and strong.

ANDY Well, I'm glad you live next door. I have a lot of trouble opening jars . . . Can I tell you about Norman Cornell?

SOPHIE Why not? Ah'm not doin' anything but countin' . . . One, two, three—

ANDY He is impulsive, compulsive, irrepressible and incorrigible . . . (SOPHIE *starts to interrupt, but* ANDY *continues*) but he is also one of the most talented, creative and inspired young writers living in this country today. Will you accept that?

SOPHIE Ah have never read anything of his except an Italian mash note in mah grocery basket . . . Four, five— (*Goes left, downstage of* ANDY, *to the desk*) Ah'm usin' the phone.

ANDY (*Rushes left*) Not until you hear me out. (*He takes the phone*) In his freshman year at Dartmouth he wrote a thesis on the economic growth of the Philippine Islands since 1930 without any previous knowledge of economics, the Philippines, or 1930.

SOPHIE There is no end to the talent of the mentally warped. (*She starts to pick up the phone, but* ANDY's *hand is there to stop her again*) If Ah have to scream, Ah'll scream.

ANDY He's been offered jobs to write for every news agency in the country, plus *Time, Look, Life,* the *Saturday Review* and the *Diners' Club Monthly.* (*He guides* SOPHIE *into the chair. He goes left upstage of* SOPHIE, *and sits on the desk*) Please believe me when I tell

37

you that Norman Cornell is not only one of the brightest young men in America today, but he is also the hope and promise of today's young generation and tomorrow's future.

(*And in the door with a mop comes the hope of tomorrow's future*)

NORMAN I just knocked your cat in the toilet. It was an accident. He's going to be all right.

(*He rushes back out, closing the door behind him*)

SOPHIE (*She rises and runs right, above the table, to the landing*) Police! Somebody get the police!

ANDY (*Running after her*) All right, Miss Rauschmeyer, let's not panic.

SOPHIE (*On the steps leading to the landing*) That's easy for you to say. He's not out flushin' your cat into the San Francisco Bay. (*She comes down the stairs*) Gimme that phone.

ANDY (*When he stops her, she starts kicking him*) I promise the minute he comes back I'll thumbtack him to the wall. Stop kicking me. I have very thin socks.

SOPHIE Either you let me call the police or Ah'll smash everything in your house, startin' with the dishes.

(*She runs into the kitchen. We hear a loud crash*)

ANDY Okay, if you want to play rough, then we'll play rough. (*We hear another crash. He charges into the kitchen after her. Now there is some yelling followed by dishes crashing, and pots and pans. Two seconds later he comes out, his arm twisted behind his back, followed by* SOPHIE, *who is doing the twisting*) All right, let go . . . I don't want to take advantage of you, so let go.

SOPHIE   Ah'm callin' the police and Ah don't want any trouble from you.

ANDY   I won't give you any trouble if you don't give me any trouble.

SOPHIE   Are you goin' to let me call the police?

ANDY   (*In pain*) Yes . . . Yes . . . (*She lets him go. He rubs his arm and goes left around the pole table.* SOPHIE *goes to the phone*) You ought to be ashamed of yourself, being stronger than a fellow.

SOPHIE   Physical fitness is as important as Godliness and Cleanliness.

ANDY   What about friendliness? And good neighborliness? Just hear me out and then if you're still upset we can go back to angriness and destructiveness. All right? (*She looks at him, then puts the phone back on the receiver*) Thank you . . . Have you ever heard of a monthly magazine called *Fallout?*

SOPHIE   Is it anything like the *Reader's Digest?*

ANDY   It is nothing like the *Reader's Digest.* It is a protest magazine. And one of the things it protests against is the *Reader's Digest* . . . What *do* you read?

SOPHIE   Ah'm a religious follower of *Sports Illustrated.*

39

ANDY Why did I ask? I'll try to explain what we do. (*He points to a sign above the bulletin board on left wall*) This is our credo—"A Remedy for a Sick Society"— (*He goes left above the pole table*) We're not doctors, we're diagnosticians. We point to the trouble spots. I'm the editor and publisher. It's my job to get it printed and sold. Norman is our staff. He is fourteen of the best writers around today. Every word, from cover to cover, is his. Besides Norman Cornell, he is sometimes Abbott Kellerman, Professor O. O. Pentergast, Gaylord Heyerdahl, José Batista, Madame Pundit Panjab, Doctor Sydney Kornheiser, Major General Wylie Krutch and Akruma Oogwana—the kid is versatile . . . Now we may use assumed names, but we believe in what we write and in what we publish. (*He gets a copy of* Fallout *from a pile of magazines under the left end of the desk*) When you go back to your room, I would like you to read last month's issue, and then I want you to tell me if you think we've spent three years and every penny we have in the world for nothing. (*He goes right, with the magazine, downstage of* SOPHIE *to below the center table*) Tell me if the things we protest against every month in *Fallout* aren't the things you protest against every day in your everyday life. (SOPHIE *starts to interrupt*) We have a modest business here, Miss Rauschmeyer. We don't make much money. If we sell every magazine we print each month, we make just enough to buy a new typewriter ribbon so we can get out the next month's issue. But we stay alive. And we love every minute of it. And we'll continue doing it as long as there is an angry breath in our body and as long as there is one single iota of corruption left in our society that's worth protesting about. (SOPHIE *makes a move to interrupt*) But, Miss Rauschmeyer, unless you smile at that talented lunatic

in there and say, "Thank you for your little Budapest sausages," one of the great organs of free press will disappear from the American scene.
(*There is a pause as he waits for her reaction*)

SOPHIE Ah don't think we've been properly introduced.

ANDY My name is Hobart, Andrew Hobart.
(*He drops the magazine on the table*)

SOPHIE (*Goes right to* ANDY) How do you do. Ah'm Sophie Rauschmeyer. (*They shake hands*) Mr. Hobart, Ah appreciate the fact that you want to preserve the dignity of our nation. As Ah told you before, Ah had the privilege of representing the United States in the Tokyo Olympics.

ANDY I think that's wonderful. How did you do?

SOPHIE Well—Ah came in fifth. Not only was Ah beaten by the USSR and Poland, but Ah also trailed behind Turkey and Egypt.

ANDY I didn't know they swam in Egypt.

SOPHIE Then you can imagine how Ah felt representing the greatest nation on earth, coming in six seconds behind a little fat girl who was raised in the desert. (*She goes left a few steps*) Since the day Ah disgraced them, Ah have not been back to mah home in Hunnicut.

ANDY Hunnicut seems to disgrace quite easily.

SOPHIE (*She comes back to the center table*) You don't

know Hunnicut. In our schools we sing all four stanzas of "The Star-Spangled Banner."

ANDY   I thought there were only three.

SOPHIE   Our principal wrote a new one. Since mah black day in Tokyo Ah have made a new life for mahself. One that Ah don't wish to jeopardize. (ANDY *goes upstage of center table to the desk, where he then sits.* SOPHIE *follows him*) Ah have found a nice job teachin' children to swim at the YWCA. (ANDY *starts licking the envelopes and then seals them*) It doesn't pay much, but it keeps me wet . . . My parents, bless 'em, come up to see me twice a year from Hunnicut. (*He nods and licks another envelope*) But most important, Ah have met, fallen in love with, and intend to marry—First Lieutenant Burt Fenneman of the United States Marines.
   (*She grabs an envelope from* ANDY, *licks it, and puts it down on the desk*)

ANDY   I'm delighted you're going to marry a Marine. I hope you live happily ever after in the halls of Montezuma.

SOPHIE   Except he's not gonna marry me if he finds that wax-moppin', cat-drownin' lunatic in mah house.

ANDY   There's a very simple solution. (*Rises*) I'll save your marriage and you'll save my magazine.

SOPHIE   How?

ANDY   (*He goes to the table and picks up a copy of* Fall-out) I promise to keep Norman away from you as much as possible, if when you see him in the hall or on the stairs you'll just smile at him. One hello from you will keep him happy for a long time. It'll keep us all happy. Will you do it?

SOPHIE   No!

ANDY   Will you do it for me?

SOPHIE   No!

ANDY   Will you do it for America?

SOPHIE   Well, if you put it that way.

ANDY   And will you please read this tonight?

SOPHIE (*She goes upstage*)   All right, but you better keep him away from me.

ANDY (*Follows*)   I promise you he'll never bother you again.
        (NORMAN *reappears with the mop*)

NORMAN (*With a big smile*)   All finished. And the cat is fine. I gave her artificial respiration.
        (*He shows how with his two index fingers, then takes the mop to the kitchen*)

SOPHIE (*She looks at* ANDY, *then back to* NORMAN *as he comes back into the room and goes to the tape recorder*) Thank you.

NORMAN (*Moved*)   Andy—she said "Thank you."

ANDY I heard.

SOPHIE Now if you'll excuse me . . .
(*She starts for the door*)

NORMAN Norman. Say my name . . . Norman.
(SOPHIE *looks at* ANDY)

ANDY (*Shrugs*) It's one little word. Norman.

SOPHIE (*Reluctantly*) Norman.

NORMAN (*He holds the mike from the tape recorder*)
Would you say it in here? I'd like to have it to keep.

SOPHIE (*She glares at* ANDY, *who looks at her for a little
understanding. She sighs.* NORMAN *turns the machine on
and she speaks into the microphone*) Norman.

NORMAN (*He turns the machine off*) Oh, that was wonderful. Thank you, Sophie.

SOPHIE (*She turns and starts out. To* ANDY) Ah've kept
mah promise. Live up to yours.
(*She exits. The instant she's gone,* NORMAN *rushes
over to the window and opens it, then rushes back
to the tape recorder*)

ANDY All right, Norman, I've just made that girl a promise.
As long as you behave decently and normally and act
like a sensible hum . . . What are you doing?

NORMAN I want the world to hear it. From her own lips.

44

Anthony Perkins and Richard Benjamin as ANDY HOBART and NORMAN CORNELL.

(*Shouts out the window*) Norman loves Sophie and someday Sophie will love . . .
(*He turns the machine on*)

SOPHIE'S VOICE (*From the recorder*)   Norman.

ANDY (*Afraid* SOPHIE *will hear*)   Turn that thing off!

NORMAN (*He stops the machine, rewinds, and shouts out the window again*)   Tell 'em again, Sophie! Who's the one who drives you out of your mind?
(*He turns the machine on*)

SOPHIE'S VOICE (*Again from the recorder*)   Norman.
(SOPHIE *bursts into the room*)

SOPHIE (*She screams and goes to the pole table*)   Ah heard that. He is using mah voice in vain. That's against the law. Make him stop.

ANDY (*Runs after her*)   He was just kidding around. He won't do it again.

NORMAN   I was just kidding around. I won't do it again.

SOPHIE   Stop embarrassin' me in front of mah neighbors. And that's the last time Ah'm warnin' you. (*She points her finger at him, and sees her fingernails*) Look at that. Now mah nails are beginnin' to crack.
(*She exits.* NORMAN *turns back to the tape recorder*)

ANDY (*He closes the door*)   If you turn that machine on again, you'll be recording your own death.

45

NORMAN I'll play it very low. She'll never hear me. (*To the machine*) Whisper it, Sophie. Tell me and nobody else. Who do you love?
(*He turns the machine on, lowering the volume*)

SOPHIE'S VOICE (*Whispering from the recorder*) Norman.
(NORMAN *falls to his knees as the curtain falls*)

Act Two

It is the next day, about 5 P.M. The room is in pretty much the same condition, though the bills have been cleaned up from the floor around the desk and the dirty cup and coffee pot have been removed from the center table. Two used coffee containers have replaced the stack of newspapers on the ratan stool. ANDY's *briefcase, the United Nations grocery bag, and the "bon voyage" basket are no longer in sight. The tape recorder is missing from the desk and the clippings as well, but the dummy magazine is still there to be finished. A recent copy of* Fallout *is on the center table. The ukelele is back on the kitchen bar. On the slant-top desk we now see two hairbrushes and an electric cordless razor. On the sofa down right is an empty coffee can. Both doors are closed on the balcony.*

There is no one on stage, but we can hear the slow, steady rhythm of a typewriter coming from NORMAN's *bedroom. It stops occasionally, then proceeds to plod on.*

The front door opens and ANDY *enters carrying a small bag, his bathing suit wrapped in a towel, and a terrycloth robe. In the other hand he carries a jar of Noxzema. He walks carefully and in pain, the result of an excruciating sunburn.*

ANDY   Norman? (*The typewriter clicks away.* ANDY *looks up at* NORMAN's *room and nods in relief. He throws the bag, towel, and robe onto the sofa, and puts the Noxzema in his jacket pocket*) I'm back! I'm back from the beach . . . I have first degree burns on ninety-eight percent of my body—the other two percent is scorched. We went a

49

half a mile out on the surfboard and there wasn't a god-damned wave for three hours . . . (*The typewriter continues*) The only time I had shade was when a bird flew over me . . . You can see his outline on my back. (*He starts up the stairs*) This is my eighth jar of Noxzema. (*The typewriter continues but no sound of* NORMAN) . . . How's it going, Norm? (*Still no answer*) Norman . . . ? (*Now he's nervous. He starts up the stairs to* NORMAN's *room*) Norman, you hear me? (*He goes into* NORMAN's *room. The typing stops.* ANDY *returns carrying the tape recorder. He takes Noxzema out of his pocket, unscrews the top and puts a dab under his shirt at the back of his neck. He winces as the cold meets the hot. He picks up the phone gingerly, then starts to dial but winces in pain after the second dial. With his left hand he takes some more Noxzema and applies it to the dialing finger of his right hand and then continues to dial. He also puts a little on his ear before applying the phone to that spot. Then he talks, in pain and softly*) Hello, Mrs. Mackininee . . . ? It's me, Andy . . . I can't speak louder, my lips won't open all the way . . . No, the chattering stopped but now I have chills. I really don't think I'll be able to come down for that cock-tail—do you mind? You *do* mind . . . Then I'll be down for that cocktail . . . (*He hangs up*) I sold my soul.

> (*The door opens and* NORMAN *steps in. He holds one hand over his eye, and he seems to be in some pain.* ANDY *looks at him*)

NORMAN (*Calmly, looking at* ANDY *through his other eye*) Why did you hit me with an apple?

ANDY   Why?

NORMAN Yes, why? Why did you hit me with an apple? (*He goes to the landing*) What were you trying to do, take my eye out?

ANDY I was trying to *kill* you but I'll take whatever I can get.

NORMAN (*Going up to the balcony*) I don't think it's funny. Do you know what the impact force is of an apple falling three-and-a-half stories? Forty-eight miles per hour. That apple was doing forty-eight miles an hour.
      (*He goes into the room*)

ANDY You're lucky you didn't get a jar of Noxzema doing seventy-five . . . ! I'm not going to ask you where you were, Norman, because I think I know where. I'm just curious as to why you came back. (NORMAN *comes out of his room, his jacket off*) Because there is nothing left for you here except physical mutilation.

NORMAN (*Comes down the stairs*) I came back because I have work to do. I believe we have a magazine to get out.
      (*He goes left toward the desk*)

ANDY (*Goes right*) Norman . . . Don't play with me. I'm in a fragile state of mind.

NORMAN If you'll excuse me—
      (NORMAN *puts a handkerchief in his pocket and sits. Next he puts a piece of paper in the typewriter*)

ANDY Who are you kidding? What about the girl?

NORMAN (*Looks straight at him*) What girl?

ANDY That star-spangled cornpone next door! I think I know where you were this morning, Norman. You were down at the delicatessen having a life-sized statue of her made in potato salad.

NORMAN You're wrong, Andy. I'm no longer interested. It's over. Done. Finished. Finito.

ANDY Is that a fact?

NORMAN That's a fact.

ANDY Then who did I hear in your room at three o'clock this morning playing "Prisoner of Love" on tissue paper and comb?

NORMAN Me! That was me! But that was last night. And last night is not today.

ANDY Something's happened, Norman, and I'm afraid to ask what. What's happened, Norman? (NORMAN *turns away from* ANDY. ANDY *goes upstage to* NORMAN's *left*) Look at me and tell me what happened!

NORMAN (*Walking away, stage right*) Nothing.

ANDY You followed her this morning.

NORMAN I don't want to talk about it.

ANDY You waited for her outside the "Y."

NORMAN (*Right of the center table*) I did not wait for her outside the "Y."

ANDY You went *inside* the "Y"?

NORMAN (*He sits on the chair*) I don't want to talk about it.

ANDY You went inside and started yelling for Sophie.

NORMAN I did not yell. I asked politely.

ANDY *Then* you started to yell and they asked you to leave.

NORMAN I don't want to talk about it.

ANDY (*He goes to the center table*) You didn't go all over the YWCA looking for her, did you?

NORMAN No, I did not go all over the YWCA looking for her.

ANDY Where *did* you look?

NORMAN Just the swimming pool.

ANDY (*He turns away*) I don't want to talk about it.

NORMAN They wear bathing suits, if that's what you're worried about.

ANDY That's what I was worried about. What did she do, threaten to call the police?

53

NORMAN She did *not* threaten to call the police.

ANDY What *did* she do?

NORMAN She *called* the police . . . They took me away in a patrol car.

ANDY I knew it. I knew it.

NORMAN (*He gets up*) You wanna hear my side?

ANDY I'm not through with *their* side yet.

NORMAN (*He sits*) We live in a police state, Andy. Did you know we are living in a police state?

ANDY (*Who can reason with this idiot*) I know. First they start burning books. Then they keep the men out of the women's pools.

NORMAN As we drove away I heard her screaming, "I hate you . . . I hate you, I loathe you, and I despise you. Hate, hate, hate, loathe, despise, and hate!" So I figured the best thing to do is forget about her.

ANDY I think you made a wise decision, Norman.

NORMAN I mean if she wants to play it cool, I don't have time to waste.

ANDY (*He may be serious*) Do you mean that, Norman?

NORMAN (*He gets up again*) I want to bury myself in work, Andy. Busy. I have to get busy again. (*He goes left, downstage of the table and* ANDY, *to the desk*) Just give me a typewriter and a lot of paper and then stand back, because you may get hurt.

(*He sits at the desk*)

ANDY   I think you really mean it. That's wonderful! (*He goes to the up left table, gets a pile of paper and hands it to* NORMAN) Here. Type. No spaces, just lots of words.

NORMAN   What did I see in her, Andy? She's not bright, you know. Do you think she's bright?

ANDY   She has a native intelligence. Of a very remote country.

NORMAN   We have absolutely nothing in common. And how long does physical attraction last?

ANDY   An hour, an hour and a half the most.

NORMAN   Say it again!

ANDY   Sophie!

NORMAN   Say the last part.

ANDY   Rauschmeyer.

NORMAN   Now the whole thing.

ANDY   Sophie Rauschmeyer!

NORMAN   You're boring me. I've got work to do.

55

ANDY (*Elated*) Ah ha! I'll knock out the mailing list. (*He goes to the up left table and gets the clipboard with pencil attached—he then goes to the chair right of the center table*) You just sit there and write. If you want to eat or drink or smoke or go to the bathroom, you sit there and I'll do everything. (NORMAN *starts to type and he goes at it furiously.* ANDY *sits and makes out the mailing list.* NORMAN *stops, looks at what he wrote, quickly tears it out of the typewriter, crumples it up, throws it away, puts another piece in and begins to type furiously. Then he stops, looks at what he wrote, tears it out of the machine, crumples it and throws it away. He then rises, paces right, sits, and puts in another sheet of paper and begins to type.* ANDY *looks up at this. The third time that* NORMAN *starts and stops typing is too much for* ANDY) Norman, if you're having trouble, maybe I can help you.

NORMAN (*Looks up at him*) What is today's date?

ANDY Norman, the date isn't important. Just write the article. I'll fill the date in later.

NORMAN (*He stares at the paper*) You're right . . . Who cares about the date? Boy, it's good to get back in harness again. (*He stares at the blank paper a moment*) And here we go . . . (*He adjusts the margin indicator*) You notice how I don't mention her name anymore?

ANDY You're not concentrating, Norman.

NORMAN You're right. You're right . . . You'd better get up on the roof because I'm opening the flood gates. Okay. We're all set . . . The paper is in—my fingers are poised . . . An idea is forming in my mind . . . Something is about to come out—

ANDY   Norman, don't announce it. You're a writer, not a train conductor.

NORMAN   Maybe if I just started typing, something'll come out.
(*He starts to type as* ANDY *looks at him incredulously*)   .

ANDY   I don't think that's going to work, Norman.

NORMAN   I can try, can't I? There's no harm in trying.
(*He types. After doing a line, he stops and looks at it*)
Andy!

ANDY (*Hopefully*)   Yes?

NORMAN   I think I'm going out of my mind.

ANDY   You're stale, sweetheart. You haven't written anything in nearly five days.

NORMAN   Did you see what I just put down on this paper?
Zizzivivizz! Second in my class at Dartmouth and I wrote zizzivivizz . . . ! You wouldn't accept work like that from a monkey.

ANDY   Don't get hysterical on me, Norman.

NORMAN (*He rips the sheet out of the typewriter and takes it to* ANDY)   Here. Read it for yourself. What does that say?

ANDY (*Resigned*) Zizzivivizz!

NORMAN (*Crumples the paper, throws it on the table and goes back to the desk*) Don't tell me not to get hysterical. Maybe if I called her at the "Y" and tried to apologize . . .

ANDY (*Rises and goes to a place above the table*) She just had the police drag you away. Does it make sense for you to call her again?

NORMAN You're talking to a man who just wrote zizzivivizz . . . ! (*He picks up the phone*) I'll dial, you talk to her.

ANDY Why should *I* talk to her?

NORMAN Because my mouth dries up when I talk to her. No words come out, just little bla bla sounds. (*He demonstrates*) Bla bla bla—

ANDY If you dial, Norman, you're going to bla bla to her yourself.

NORMAN (*Glares at him, the phone still in hand*) You know what you are, Hobart? You're cold turkey. Cold turkey, lumpy stuffing, and watery cranberry sauce. You have all the romance and sensitivity of a used-car lot. (*He dials*) You know what else you are? You're a sexual snob. You don't get really excited unless the girl has a straight-A average . . . Tell the truth, Andy, the sexiest woman who ever lived was Madame Curie, right?

58

ANDY   Right. I dream of her leaning over a low-cut micro-
scope.

NORMAN   I don't need you. I'll talk to Sophie myself.
(*Into the phone*) Hello? Is this the YWCA . . . ? It
is? Bla—bla—bla—bla . . .
      (*He quickly gives the phone to* ANDY *and goes stage
center*)

ANDY   (*Reluctantly talks into the phone*)   Miss Sophie
Rauschmeyer, please . . . What? (NORMAN *hurries to*
ANDY'*s side to listen*) When . . . ? Why . . . ? Where?

NORMAN   (*Anxiously*)   What - when - why - where - what?
What's happening?

ANDY   I see. Thank you. (*He hangs up*) They just fired
her! They said it's the *third* time this week a madman
caused a commotion there.
      (*We hear a pounding on the door*)

SOPHIE'S VOICE (*Offstage*)   Open this door or so help me,
Ah'll break it down.

NORMAN   Andy, help me. What'll I do?

ANDY   Get out of here. Let me talk to her.
      (*The doorbell buzzes furiously*)

NORMAN (*Starting upstairs*)   What will you say, Andy?
What will you tell her?

ANDY   She's banging on the door. I can't audition for you
now.
      (*Again the doorbell buzzes angrily*)

NORMAN (*Halfway upstairs*)   Just tell me one thing. Tell me one nice thing you're going to say about me.

ANDY   You never wear brown shoes with a blue suit. (*The doorbell again*) Get out of here . . . (NORMAN *is climbing the ladder to the roof*) Where are you going?

NORMAN   On the roof. If everything is all right, call me and I'll come down. If not, I'll jump down.
> (*He disappears through door at the top of ladder. The doorbell buzzes again.* ANDY *goes to the door and opens it.* SOPHIE *enters—wet. She carries a YWCA duffle bag and a copy of* Fallout)

SOPHIE (*She goes to the foot of the stairs*)   Where is he? Where is that insane, crazy, trespassin' lunatic? (ANDY *closes the door*) Ah know exactly what Ah'm goin' to do to him. Ah planned it all as Ah sat there drippin' all over the bus.

ANDY (*Goes toward her*)   He's up on the roof, miserable and eating his heart out.

SOPHIE   Well, you can tell him not to bother. Ah'm gonna get a big dog to eat it out for him . . . Ah have been fired. They didn't even give me time to dry off.

ANDY   I know. I just spoke to the "Y." But it wasn't your fault. Didn't you explain that to them?

SOPHIE   Ah found it difficult gettin' their attention while a crazy man was chasin' me all through the YWCA . . . And that present of his is still pecking away at everyone in the buildin'.

ANDY   What present?

SOPHIE   The duck. He brought me a live duck. It's still there quackin' and snappin' at everyone. When Ah left, the gym teacher was a-hangin' from the basketball hoop and then that crazy bird chased a seventy-three-year-old arts and crafts teacher down to the swimmin' pool and off the high diving board.

ANDY   I didn't know about that.

SOPHIE   Well, did you know that Ah've been locked out of mah apartment until Ah pay mah rent which Ah can't do because Ah don't have a job.

ANDY   Look, we'll make it up to you somehow. I'll get you another job. Just give me a couple of days.

SOPHIE (*Goes left, downstage of* ANDY)   Ah don't have a couple of days. Ah have rent to pay and food to buy. What am Ah gonna do?

ANDY   There must be someone in San Francisco who needs somebody young and healthy and strong . . . I don't suppose you've ever considered professional football?

SOPHIE (*She goes downstage to the phone on the desk and starts to dial*)   Ah'm callin' my fiancé!

ANDY (*He goes toward* SOPHIE)   Wait . . . I have an idea. I don't say you're going to love it, but how would you like to come to work for us?

SOPHIE   Ah would rather get beaten in the Olympics by Red China.

61

ANDY   Why not? It'll pay your rent and buy you your iron and steel, or whatever it is you eat.

SOPHIE (*She hangs up*)   Ah believe you're serious. If you're serious, Ah suggest you make yourself available for our country's mental health program. Do you think Ah would work for that bomb aimed at the heart of America?

ANDY   What bomb?

SOPHIE (*She goes a few steps right to* ANDY)   Mr. Hobart, Ah don't know if you're a communist, or a fascist, or just a plain old-fashioned traitor—but you are certainly no American.

ANDY   What are you calling me a traitor for?

SOPHIE (*She picks up the magazine from the pole table*) For this! For holding your country up to ridicule in black and white. All Ah read last night was the table of contents, but if you don't like the country that gave you your birth, why don't you go back where you came from?

ANDY   I don't know what you're talking about, but writing constructive criticism about the degenerating American way of life is certainly not treason.

SOPHIE   Ah don't know what is in your government-overthrowing mind, but do you expect me to work for a magazine that publishes an article entitled (*Goes right, upstage of* ANDY, *and looks through the pages*) . . . "Is LBJ on LSD?"

ANDY   We are not implying that he takes drugs. It's a symbolic alliteration meaning maybe the President in certain areas has gone too far.

SOPHIE   How about "Twenty-Seven Ways to Burn a Wet Draft Card"? Written from personal experience, Mr. Hobart?

ANDY   For your information, I happened to have served two years in the United States Army where I was interpreter for Brigadier General Walker Cooper.

SOPHIE   In what country?

ANDY   In *this* country. That idiot could hardly speak English! (*Tosses the magazine on the table*) My feelings about this country run just as deeply as yours, but if you'll turn down the national anthem for a few minutes, you'll be able to hear what some of the people are complaining about.

SOPHIE   Well, Ah am one of the people and *you* are one of the things Ah'm complaining about.

ANDY   Well, fortunately, you're not in much of a position to complain about *anything* . . . ! Look, if you don't work, you don't eat. If you don't eat, you get very skinny, you fall down and then you're dead. (*He goes left, upstage of the pole table*) If you think your Marine will be happy living with a dead, skinny lady, that's his business. Personally, I think you ought to accept the meager bread I'm offering you.

SOPHIE   First you take away my loaf and then you offer me your meager bread.

ANDY   Why does everything you say sound like it came out of the Bible?

SOPHIE   Thank goodness you heard of the book.

ANDY   Look, do you want the job or don't you? If you don't want it, *I'll* take it, 'cause I need the money.

SOPHIE   Unfortunately, so do Ah. Just tell me why . . . why do you want me around here?

ANDY   I'll tell you why. I *don't* want you around here. But that nut up on the hot tin roof wants you around here. You believe in your principles, I believe in mine. Mine is this magazine, and I'll do anything to keep it from going under water—that was an unfortunate choice of phrase.

SOPHIE   All right. That's your principle. Mah principle is breathin', eatin' and livin', just like any other animal on this earth.

ANDY   So much for your character references. Now about salary. What did you get at the "Y"?

SOPHIE   Seventy-two dollars.

ANDY   Norman and I both know how to swim; I'll give you fifty-five.

SOPHIE   For fifty-five dollars Ah will come in early and poison your coffee. Ah want what Ah got at the "Y." Seventy-two dollars.

64

ANDY (*Reluctantly*)   So be it, you're hired. Your hours will be from ten to six, half a day on Saturday. Can you type?

SOPHIE   No.

ANDY   Can you take shorthand?

SOPHIE   No.

ANDY   Can you do filing?

SOPHIE   No.

ANDY   Maybe you'd better come in at eleven . . . Can you cook?

SOPHIE   Mah cat seems to think so.

ANDY   Okay, you can make lunches and pretend to look busy. Let's say you have two main functions. First, to keep out of my way at all times, and second, to *smile* at Norman as much as is humanly possible.

SOPHIE   Yes, sir. The first Ah will do with the utmost dedication. And the second Ah will do over mah dead body.

ANDY (*Goes right, downstage of* SOPHIE)   Miss Rauschmeyer, it's evident you and I haven't gotten along since you came to work here . . . We're both trying to make the best out of an impossible situation. You need money, I need you to say goo-goo to my partner once in a while. Now I suggest you roll up your lips and smile so we can get to work.

65

SOPHIE   All right, Ah'll make mah bargain with the devil. Ah've never run from a fight. Ah'm ready to go to work. (*She extends her hand*)

ANDY   Am I supposed to shake that?

SOPHIE   No, you're supposed to put seventy-two dollars in it.

ANDY   We pay at the end of the week. Company policy.

SOPHIE   Then Ah'll start at the end of the week. Ah-don't-trust-you policy.

ANDY   All right, wait a minute. (*He gets the milk bottles filled with pennies*) There's seventy dollars in pennies. (*He gives her the two bottles, takes the third bottle and empties some of it in the can on the sofa*) Minus Federal withholding tax and social security.
    (*Curtain. While the curtain is down, we hear the sound of a typewriter over the house speakers*)

It is a few days later.

Missing from the room now is SOPHIE's *YWCA bag, all the crumpled paper from the floor, the coffee can seen on the sofa in the previous scene, the Noxzema jar, and all of* ANDY's *beach equipment. Half a dozen books are now occupying the shelf where the pennies were. The left side of the center table is set for lunch. A copy of* Sports Illustrated *is also on the table.*

NORMAN *is seated at the typewriter, his back to the front door. He is pounding away like a man obsessed. To his right, on the desk, is a pile of typed yellow pages. Despite this display of frenetic labor,* NORMAN *seems to be a happy man. Suddenly he stops as he seems stuck on something. He thinks a moment, then picks up a bell that is on top of his typed pages, and rings it with a flourish.*

SOPHIE *appears from the kitchen wearing a little apron over a bright orange dress and holding a dish towel. She looks at him.*

NORMAN   Ubiquitous.

SOPHIE (*She goes left to the slanting desk where there is a large dictionary. She looks up the word*)   Ubiquitous. U-b-i-q-u-i-t-o-u-s. Ubiquitous.
   (*She closes the dictionary and marches back to the kitchen*)

NORMAN   Thank you.

67

SOPHIE   You're welcome.
> (*She smiles, then exits. Once* SOPHIE *is in the kitchen,* NORMAN *rises, goes to the slanting desk, gets the dictionary and brings it to his desk. He sits at the typewriter again and rings the bell.* SOPHIE *returns, tired, carrying the bowl with the mixing spoon*)

NORMAN   Meretricious!
> (*Wordlessly* SOPHIE *crosses left to the slanting desk, but discovers that the dictionary has been moved to* NORMAN'*s left. She quickly runs through the pages, stops and reads from the book, slowly and deliberately*)

SOPHIE   Meretricious. M-e-r-e-t-r-i-c-i-o-u-s! Meretricious!
> (*She puts the dictionary back on the desk, picks up her mixing bowl and starts to exit. Once past him, she turns and gives him a huge, forced smile baring all her teeth. She continues to the kitchen. He picks up the bell again and rings with a flourish. She turns around*) Stop ringin' that bell, Ah'm not a cow!

NORMAN   Well, you don't like it when I call you Sophie.

SOPHIE   Ah'm an employee here, mah name is Miss Rauschmeyer . . . What is it, Mr. Cornell?

NORMAN   What's for lunch, Miss Rauschmeyer?

SOPHIE   Banana fritters, Mr. Cornell. Do you like them?

NORMAN   I love them. What are they?

68

Connie Stevens as SOPHIE RAUSCHMEYER.

SOPHIE   Fritters made with bananas.
>   (*She starts to go back into the kitchen, stops, turns and smiles. Then exits.* NORMAN *rushes to the slant-top desk and quickly combs his hair, looking in the mirror on the wall above the desk. He quickly shaves with an electric cordless razor. Then he goes toward the kitchen*)

NORMAN   Do you notice the way I've calmed down? (*He looks in*) I'll never know how we got along without a secretary all these—oh, let me help you with that.
>   (*He goes into the kitchen. We hear* SOPHIE *shout and then a loud crash.* NORMAN *rushes out and goes stage right*)

SOPHIE   (*Following him, brandishing a pot*)   You try that with your hands again and you'll have to learn to type with your nose.

NORMAN   Your apron was slipping. I was just tying it in the back.

SOPHIE   And stop trying to get me into corners.

NORMAN   I'm not trying to get you into corners.

SOPHIE   Then how come this mornin' for ten minutes we had our heads stuck in the oven?

NORMAN   All right, don't be angry. Don't be mad at me. (*Goes back to the desk*) You go back into the kitchen and I'll go back to work. See? See? I'm working again. (*He types*) See? Working . . . (*She returns to the kitchen and after a moment of disgust, he resumes work.*

69

He is once more engrossed and does not hear or notice ANDY *as he comes in the front door.* ANDY *looks exhausted from his outside activities. He looks over at* NORMAN, *whose back is to him, typing away feverishly.* ANDY *tiptoes behind him to get a better look at his work without disturbing him. He reads over* NORMAN's *shoulder a minute. He seems pleased with what he reads. To get a better look, he leans over and places his hands on* NORMAN's *shoulders.* NORMAN *closes his eyes upon feeling the hand on his shoulder. He turns his head and kisses* ANDY's *hand)* Forgive me! *(He notices that it is* ANDY's *hand and jumps out of his chair and turns angrily to* ANDY) Are you crazy? You wanna give me a heart attack? Don't ever sneak up on me like that again.

ANDY I didn't want to disturb you. You've really been working, heh?
     (He picks up a stack of typewritten pages and begins to look them over)

NORMAN I've been doing fine, fine.

ANDY *(Looks around)* Where's Esther Williams?
     (He starts walking stage left, followed by NORMAN)

NORMAN *(Following)* Shhh! I thought you were going to be gone all day.

ANDY I couldn't take anymore. *(Turns and now walks stage right, followed by* NORMAN) I just flew under the Golden Gate Bridge with a crazy landlady pilot. Actually she did very well for a woman who just got her license yesterday.
     (He continues to read NORMAN's *pages)*

70

NORMAN   Tell me all about it later. I want to finish this.

ANDY   She made three passes at the bridge. On the third one we had to pay a toll. (*He starts up the stairs*) Norman, this is good. It's better than good. It's brilliant.

NORMAN   I know . . . I know . . .
> (ANDY *goes on up the stairs and into his room.* SOPHIE *comes out of the kitchen carrying a frying pan with a banana fritter*)

SOPHIE   Come on! Here's your lunch. Eat it while it's hot.
> (NORMAN *crosses and sits in a chair to the left of the table—he tucks a napkin in his shirt*)

NORMAN   I like that. You're worried about me.
> (SOPHIE *tosses the fritter onto the plate already set on the table and returns to the kitchen. She re-enters, taking off her apron*)

SOPHIE   (*Standing above the table*)   Would that be all now? If so, Ah'd like to go home.

NORMAN   You could vacuum the rug.

SOPHIE   Where's the vacuum?

NORMAN   In that closet. (SOPHIE *leaves her apron on the kitchen bar en route to the closet*) I'll help you with it. It's very heavy.
> (*He goes into the closet after her and closes the door. We hear a loud crash. The closet door opens and* SOPHIE *comes storming out. She slams the door behind her.* NORMAN *does not appear.* ANDY *rushes*

out of his room without his jacket and comes running down the stairs)

SOPHIE   This time Ah'm pressin' charges.
(*She heads for the door*)

ANDY (*Carrying* NORMAN's *yellow pages*)   What's the matter? Where's Norman?

SOPHIE   You'll find him under the vacuum cleaner.
(*She storms out and slams the door.* NORMAN *comes out of the closet, holding his head in pain and wearing the vacuum-cleaner hose around his neck*)

ANDY (*To* NORMAN)   What did you do?

NORMAN   I bit her earlobe! It was dangling right in front of my mouth. What did you want me to do, ignore it?

ANDY (*He rushes to the door and goes out in the hall and shouts*)   Miss Rauschmeyer! Sophie! Wait a minute!

NORMAN (*Follows* ANDY *to the door*)   Tell her I'm sorry.

ANDY   Seventy-five dollars! I'll raise your salary to seventy-five dollars a week. (*He comes back into the room and leaves the door open*) She's coming back.

NORMAN (*Following* ANDY)   Andy, you've got to square me with her just one more time.

ANDY   Norman, this has got to stop. She's becoming one of the highest-priced secretaries in America—and she can't even type.

NORMAN Tell her I've been working under a great strain lately. That I haven't been myself. Help me! What am I gonna do?

ANDY (*Removes the napkin and the vacuum hose from* NORMAN's *neck and tosses them upstage of the kitchen bar*) Go downstairs and buy a bottle of wine. We'll have a party just for the three of us.

NORMAN (*He rushes to the front door*) That's a wonderful idea. I'll get a bottle of muscatel.

ANDY Not muscatel. Champagne. Girls love champagne.

NORMAN That's right. I'll take all my pennies and get a bottle of champagne.
  (*He starts toward the shelf where the pennies were kept*)

ANDY (*He grabs* NORMAN, *stops him and shoves him toward the door*) No, you're right. Muscatel is better. Now get out of here.
  (NORMAN *gets to the door just as* SOPHIE *returns.* NORMAN *hides his face with his hands*)

NORMAN Sophie, I just want to say. I know you hate me now, but—bla bla bla bla bla . . .
  (*He runs down the corridor and disappears.* SOPHIE *ignores him*)

SOPHIE Where's mah three-dollar raise?

ANDY You'll be drinking it in ten minutes.

73

SOPHIE   Ah knew Ah shouldn't have trusted you.
(*She turns to go*)

ANDY   I thought you never run from a fight.

SOPHIE (*Turning back*)   Ah don't. Ah just had one in the closet. Mah ear is pierced now and Ah don't even wear earrings.

ANDY   I told you it wouldn't be easy. I should have known you didn't have the guts to stick it out.

SOPHIE   Stick it out? Ah have been smiling at that idiot for three days. (*She gives a big, forced smile as she comes back into the room to the center table*) You see that? That's what Ah've been doing since ten o'clock this morning.

ANDY   Well, cut it out. You look like a demented ventriloquist.
(*He picks up* NORMAN's *work and sits to the right of the table—he takes a pencil from the mug*)

SOPHIE   Look, this was not *mah* stupid idea. It was *your* stupid idea.

ANDY   Well, it's a very *smart* stupid idea because it's working!
(*He flourishes* NORMAN's *papers in the air as proof*)

SOPHIE   It's working for *you!* You're gettin' your magazine. Ah'm gettin' holes in mah ears.

ANDY   I happen to be paying through the nose for those holes in your ears. It won't happen again . . . Now I've got fifty pages to edit so I'd like a little quiet, please.

SOPHIE You won't even know Ah'm here—'cause Ah won't be here!
(*She starts for the door*)

ANDY (*Turns and shouts*) You'll be here because I'm paying you to be here and he's coming back in ten minutes and he *wants* you here.

SOPHIE (*Closes the door and comes downstage*) Then *here* Ah will be!
(*She sits left of the table angrily, grabs a magazine, crosses her legs, and reads*)

ANDY (*Looks at her*) This is not the Christian Science Reading Room. It's an office. And there's work to be done.

SOPHIE Then do it.
(*She continues reading*)

ANDY I'm talking about you.

SOPHIE Would you like me to type a letter? Ah can have it finished a year from September.

ANDY You can sharpen some pencils—and be quiet.

SOPHIE Yes, Boss!
(SOPHIE *glares at him, then gets up and goes to the radiator where there's a pencil sharpener. From a bowl she takes one, inserts it in the sharpener, and grinds. It makes a loud noise.* ANDY *looks up, then goes over to her*)

ANDY What are you doing?

75

SOPHIE   What you told me to do.

ANDY (*Pulls the pen from the sharpener*)   Thank you. I now have a ballpoint pen without a ballpoint. (*He goes to a tall vase on the kitchen bar and takes a feather duster from it. He goes back toward* SOPHIE) Do you see this?

SOPHIE   Ah see it.

ANDY   First let me tell you that it is not a dead chicken on a stick. It's a feather duster. By that I don't mean you dust feathers with it. You hold it on this end (*He demonstrates*)—and you flick it against the furniture, thus dusting it. Do you think you could do that?

SOPHIE   Lefty or righty?

ANDY   If you'd like, you can stick it in your pierced ear and shake your head. Just clean the room and be quiet.
      (*He puts the duster on the pole table, then goes back and sits in a chair to continue working.* SOPHIE *glares at him, holding the duster*)

SOPHIE   Yes, sir! (*She begins to dust the pole table, vigorously and angrily—she knocks magazines onto the floor. She dusts her way across the room to* ANDY'S *chair, dusts under it, making some noise. Then she moves back to the center table*) Ah think Ah'm gettin' the hang of it.

ANDY   Yes, you seem to be.

SOPHIE (*She dusts bits of torn paper out of the ashtray, and sings as she goes up to the kitchen bar*)

76

"Yankee doodle went to town, riding on a pony,
Stuck a feather in his cap and called it macaroni . . ."
(Now she is dusting the steps leading to the landing)

ANDY You're not going to whistle the second chorus, are you?

SOPHIE Ah just work here. Ah do what Ah'm told.
(She starts to whistle. ANDY gets up and crosses to her. He takes her wrist, leads her to the desk)

ANDY All right. *(He takes some envelopes from the end of the desk and some stamps and places them before her)* Here are fifty addressed envelopes and fifty stamps. You have a tongue. Don't talk. Lick.
(He takes the duster from her and puts it on the pole table. He goes back to the chair and picks up the pages)

SOPHIE *(Seated at the desk, holding the envelopes)* Are these announcements for next week's cell meeting, Comrade?

ANDY No. Actually they're very thin bombs. You just add water. *(She laughs. Then she begins to lick the stamps and places them on the envelopes)* I get the impression that you don't approve of me as a person.

SOPHIE If that's what you are, that's what Ah don't.

ANDY Why not?

SOPHIE Because Ah don't approve of your character, your

77

philosophy, your principles, your ideals, your vocation, your methods, your scruples—shall Ah continue?

ANDY   Look, your opinions on anything have as much practical value as a 1939 calendar. I'm not paying seventy-five dollars a week to listen to a limited vocabulary. Be quiet and lick the stamps. I'm a busy man.
(*He goes back to his pages*)

SOPHIE   So was John Wilkes Booth the night he assassinated Lincoln.

ANDY (*Stops*)   Are you implying I was in on the Lincoln job?

SOPHIE   Ah'm talking about your present activities. But Ah wouldn't put it past you.

ANDY   Sorry, that night I was in Philadelphia cracking the Liberty Bell. (*He gathers his papers, rises, and starts up the stairs*) I can't concentrate in front of the Senate Investigating Committee.

SOPHIE   The truth is always difficult to face. (*She stands up*) Can mah tongue rest? The well has dried up.

ANDY (*He stops on the stairs*)   Look—if you're unhappy here, why don't you take a job as night watchman at the Statue of Liberty? Then you could swim around her at night checking to see if the torch went out.

SOPHIE (*Going upstage a few steps*)   "The enforcers of justice have always been the scapegoat of the enemies of freedom . . ." Do you know where Ah read that?

78

ANDY   On the back of a Patrick Henry bubble-gum card?

SOPHIE (*She walks stage left above the pole table*)   No—
in the speeches of Socrates. Did you ever read the
speeches of Socrates?

ANDY   I'm waiting for the paperback to come out.
(*He goes up to the balcony*)

SOPHIE (*Shouts up*)   It's out. That's where Ah read it . . .
It would shock you, Mr. Hobart, to know the amount
of political literature Ah have read.

ANDY   I would be nonplussed if you got into anything
deeper than the names and addresses of the girls in the
Miss America Contest. I notice that your tongue is functioning again. Go back and lick the stamps.
(*He goes into his room*)

SOPHIE   And Ah'm sure if it was left up to a *traitor* like
you, no one would *win* the Miss America Contest.
(*She goes back to the desk and stamp-licking—standing up.* ANDY *comes out of his room again, much
angrier at the "traitor" remark*)

ANDY   You're right. I think a parade of pretty girls is fine.
But listening to Miss North Dakota singing an aria from
The Barber of Seville in the key of M, while baking an
upside-down seven-layer cake in a hoop skirt she hooped
herself, is beyond human endurance . . . I'll be very
frank with you, Miss Rauschmeyer, up until now I'm not
happy with your work.
(*He goes back to his room*)

79

SOPHIE (*She glares after him. She is murmuring to herself and what she says is almost inaudible*) Ah suppose next he'll outlaw apple pie.

ANDY (*He comes out of his room*) I heard that. I happen to love apple pie. Which, for your information, originated in Bavaria, Germany.

SOPHIE (*She goes stage left to above the pole table*) That's a lie. Apple pie is as American as blueberry pie.

ANDY The only truly indigenous American foods are Thanksgiving turkey and chicken chow mein. (*He starts down the stairs as she goes right to meet him*) You're deliberately distracting me from working on my magazine, aren't you?

SOPHIE (*Returning left to the desk, and back to the stamps*) Each citizen must do what he can.

ANDY Of all the bigoted things—you haven't read one word in it past the table of contents.

SOPHIE You don't have to drink the poison if it says so on the label.

ANDY I'm going in the closet to work. Call me when Norman gets back.
(*He goes up center*)

SOPHIE (*She goes toward him*) All right, tell me. Is there *anything* about this country you do like?

ANDY I like almost everything about this country except people who like *absolutely everything* about this country.

SOPHIE   Why don't you answer mah question?

ANDY   Why don't you question my answer?

SOPHIE   Why don't you talk like a person so Ah can understand which are the questions and which are the answers?

ANDY   Would it be all right if I worked in your apartment?

SOPHIE   It would not. If there's gonna be a fight, let's draw the battle lines on the field of the aggressor. And don't bother guessin' who said that 'cause Ah made it up mahself.

ANDY   I had it narrowed down to you or Winston Churchill.
   (*He goes right a few steps*)

SOPHIE   (*Follows*)   *And* for your information, did you know Winston Churchill's mother was born in the United States—*in Brooklyn!*

ANDY   You'd never know it from the way he talked. (*Goes to the door, downstage of* SOPHIE) Why don't you go back to your apartment and make some chitlins or grits? Your cat must be hungry.
   (*He opens the door for her*)

SOPHIE   (*She sits right of the table*)   Ah'm not leavin' until you admit you are snide, smug, and narrow-minded.

ANDY   Will you settle for belligerent?

SOPHIE   Ah will accept deceitful and treacherous.

ANDY (*He slams the door, and comes downstage to the bottom step*) Okay, I'm deceitful and treacherous. And *you* are provincial, and old-fashioned, antiquated, unrealistic, unimaginative, unenlightened, uninformed, and unbelievably unable to understand anything that isn't under water . . . (SOPHIE *rises*) Your big trouble in life is that you were born a hundred and fifty years too late. You should have been at Bunker Hill loading muskets, raising flags, and waiting for the British to show up with the whites of their eyes. Well, you may be shocked to learn that this is 1967 and this country has a whole new set of problems. But you wouldn't know about that because I don't think you're a real person of flesh and blood with feelings and sensitivities. I don't think you could be capable of having a genuine emotional attachment for another human being unless it was first passed by Congress and amended to the Constitution and painted red, white, and blue. If you've been listening carefully, Miss Rauschmeyer, I have just made a point.

SOPHIE (*She walks to the door, opens it, then slams it shut*) All right, if you wanna make points, then Ah'm gonna make one. Ah'm gonna make the biggest point you ever heard.

ANDY (*He goes to the sofa and tosses the pages on it*) When you get to it, raise your right hand. With you it's hard to tell.

SOPHIE You'll *know* when Ah'm makin' it only you're not gonna like it. Are you listenin'?

ANDY With one ear. That's all I need with you.

SOPHIE   Then here goes. (*She comes downstage to* ANDY)
Ah don't like you for a lot of the reasons Ah already said.
But the main reason Ah don't like you is because Ah am
ingaged to Lieutenant Burt Fenneman of the United
States Marines. And in a few weeks we're supposed to
get married. But for some insane reason that only a Hun-
garian psychoanalyst could explain, Ah have suddenly
discovered—and here comes the part Ah was telling you
about—that *Ah am physically attracted to you . . . !*
Now how do you like *that* for a point? (*And she storms
out slamming the door behind her.* ANDY *does not react.
He just stands there. Suddenly the door flings open again
and* SOPHIE *stands there glaring at him, hands on her
hips*) Did you hear what Ah said?

ANDY (*Without emotion*)   I heard. I heard what you said.

SOPHIE (*Slams the door*)   Well, how do you like them
apples?

ANDY   *Those* apples.

SOPHIE (*She goes to stand above the center table*)   *Them*
apples. How do you like them?

ANDY   Are you serious?

SOPHIE (*Yelling*)   Of course Ah'm serious! There is something about your physical presence that appeals to me—
and Ah am as repulsed by it as you are.

ANDY   You couldn't possibly be.

SOPHIE   There is no earthly reason why Ah should like

83

anything about you. And Ah don't. But Ah do! What do we do about it?

ANDY   If you're looking for another boost in salary, this is *not* the way to get it.
   (*He starts up the stairs*)

SOPHIE   Where are you goin'?

ANDY   To get Norman's copy of Krafft-Ebbing. You're a bigger nut than he is.

SOPHIE   You don't believe me.

ANDY   I *believe* you. I just don't *understand* you. (*Comes back down the steps*) What do you mean you're physically attracted to me?

SOPHIE   Do you want a complete rundown of arms, legs, hair, and teeth? Go get a pencil and paper and we'll take it item for item.

ANDY   You mean you like the way I look?

SOPHIE   Not terribly.

ANDY   You like the way I walk?

SOPHIE   Not really.

ANDY   You like the way I dress?

SOPHIE   Not remotely.

84

ANDY   Then what *do you like?*

SOPHIE   *Ah like the way you smell!!*
(ANDY *turns and looks to heaven or anyone else for some help*)

ANDY   Oh, Sophie, Sophie, Sophie!

SOPHIE   And don't call me Sophie-Sophie-Sophie. Ah'm attracted to you but Ah still don't like you.

ANDY   That's impossible.

SOPHIE   Ah know. You are the most irritating, nauseating man Ah have ever met in mah life—and if you tried to kiss me right now Ah would not stop you. You wanna work on that for a while?

ANDY   (*He turns in despair and goes to the landing*)   No, I think I need outside help.

SOPHIE   Ah suppose you wanna know what started it all?

ANDY   (*Turns to a wall and just faces it*)   No, I don't.

SOPHIE   Yes, you do.

ANDY   Yes, I do. What started it all?

SOPHIE   It was your grey eyelashes. Ah have never met a man in your age bracket with grey eyelashes. Ah think it's *dumb* to have grey eyelashes, but Ah'm very glad you have them . . . Now can Ah ask you a question?

ANDY   Yes, you may ask me a question.

SOPHIE   Do you have any desire whatsoever to touch me?

ANDY   What does that mean?

SOPHIE   Which is the part you don't understand, desire or touchin'?

ANDY (*Goes downstage*)   I understand both parts, I just never thought about it.

SOPHIE (*Follows*)   Well, *think* about it . . . Time's up! Do you want to touch me or don't you?

ANDY   You've been spiking your fritters with bourbon, haven't you?

SOPHIE   Ah am being honest with mah emotions because that's the only way Ah know how to deal with them. (*She moves closer to* ANDY) The plain disgustin' truth is Ah would like to stand very close to you and feel your breath somewhere on mah neck.

ANDY   You shouldn't tell me that.

SOPHIE   Ah know it but it just comes out. Is there any possibility of you havin' the same disgustin' feeling about me?

ANDY   If I did it wouldn't be disgusting, and if I found it disgusting I wouldn't have the feeling.

SOPHIE   Ah don't think Ah got that but touché anyway.

86

ANDY (*As he moves into the right corner*) And will you stop following me around the room.

SOPHIE Ah'm not followin' you. You're runnin' from *me!*

ANDY I'm running because you're following. Stay over there!

SOPHIE Ah can't *smell* you from over here!

ANDY (*Exasperated*) What am I going to do with you?

SOPHIE Ah gave you a suggestion, you didn't do it.

ANDY Listen, you, for an all-American girl with a complete set of Eagle Scout principles, how do you explain being engaged to one man and attracted to another man?

SOPHIE Very simple explanation. Ah can't explain it.

ANDY What about your fiancé?

SOPHIE He can't explain it either.

ANDY You mean you *told* him?

SOPHIE Certainly Ah told him. We're ingaged.

ANDY Oh, God, I'm afraid to ask what his reaction was.

SOPHIE You may well fear. He wants to kill you.

ANDY WHY? WHAT DID I DO?

SOPHIE   What did Ah do when that lunatic friend of yours chased me all over the YWCA? It's nobody's fault. It's something that just happened.

ANDY (*He escapes from her by going left, between the right chair and the center table*)   Well, make it *un*happen. If I'm going to get killed by a man in uniform, let it be the enemy.

SOPHIE   Ah am tryin' just as hard as Ah can to make it unhappen. The minute you do anything physically repulsive, we'll all be a lot better off. (ANDY *looks at her and then in an effort to be physically repulsive, he knocks over the director's chair and goes to her, grabs her and gives her a hard, vicious kiss. Then he pushes her back and returns to stage left. He looks at her*) Ah liked it. We're in big trouble.

ANDY   What do you mean, *we're* in big trouble? *I'm* the one who's in big trouble.

SOPHIE   Are you going to yell at me or are you going to do something about our predicament?

ANDY (*Yelling*)   I'm going to yell at you! You're going to ruin everything I ever worked for in my entire life! Why don't you go back into the ocean with the rest of the fish? (*She smiles*) What are you smiling at?

SOPHIE   Ah like it when you yell at me?

ANDY   I don't care what you like, WHAT ARE WE GO-ING TO DO?

88

SOPHIE   How should *Ah* know? But until we think of somethin', why don't you kiss me again?
(ANDY *charges at her with a threatening finger*)

ANDY   You are without a doubt—the most—you—ah—oh, the hell with it.
(*He goes to her, takes her in his arms, and kisses her. He's not quite sure why, but at this point his common sense is beyond all reasoning.* SOPHIE *puts her arms around his neck and solidifies the kiss. The door flies open and* NORMAN *springs in happily, a bottle of muscatel in a brown paper bag in his hand*)

NORMAN   (*Singing*)   "She loves me, but . . ." (*He stops and freezes as he catches them in the embrace. He looks at* ANDY *and* SOPHIE) The least you could have done was chipped in for the wine!

Curtain

Act Three

*It is the next day, early afternoon. There is one open
suitcase, downstage of the kitchen bar. A duffle bag is on
the sofa next to the portable typewriter, all ready to go. The
luncheon dishes have been cleared and the feather duster
returned to the kitchen bar. The stamped envelopes and the
manuscript pages are no longer on the desk, but the dummy
magazine is still there, unfinished. The telephone is back
on the pole table along with a large pile of magazines near
the pole. Upstage, unseen by the audience, is an eight-pack
of empty Coke bottles.* ANDY's *clipboard is on the center
table.*

NORMAN *appears from his room at the top of the stairs,
carrying a pile of books. He leans over the railing and drops
the books like a load of bombs into the open suitcase below.*

The front door opens and ANDY, *in his raincoat, enters,
a very morose-looking young man. He looks up at* NORMAN,
who tosses his head. NORMAN *is trying to convey all his
anger and bitterness in this one gesture.*

The telephone rings. ANDY *closes the door, crosses to the
pole table and answers the phone.*

ANDY (*Into the phone*) Cavanaugh's Crematorium . . .
Oh—Mrs. Mackininee—no, I'm not trying to avoid you. I
have a little answering service on the side . . . Yes, I
called you earlier because I was wondering if I could beg
off tonight's karate party . . . Well, I'm sure the *Tako-
shimo's* are a lot of fun, but I'm awfully tired—I just
don't think I'm up to an entire evening of being thrown
against the wall . . .

> (NORMAN *comes out of his room carrying an enor-
> mous five-foot-square blowup photograph of Albert
> Einstein*)

NORMAN (*Not to* ANDY *directly*) Railway Express will pick it up in the morning.
(*He leans the picture-face to the wall and goes back into his room*)

ANDY (*Back into the phone*) Mrs. Mackininee, I definitely don't think I can make it tonight. I have some urgent business here . . . No, I'm positive I can't—Mrs. Mackininee, I think this is hardly the time to discuss a rent increase . . . Well, for that matter, I couldn't even pay a fifteen percent *decrease* . . . ! All right, if that's how you feel about it, you can pick up your apartment in the morning.
(*He hangs up.* NORMAN *comes out of his bedroom carrying a flower box with a few tiny leaves starting to sprout. He carries it down the stairs*)

NORMAN I'm taking the marijuana plant.
(*He puts the plant on the kitchen bar. He starts for the stairs again*)

ANDY Is this your final decision?

NORMAN (*He crosses to the tape recorder, turns it on, picks up the speaker and switches on to record*) It's my final decision. This is a recording.
(*He switches it off and starts up right*)

ANDY Because I think you're making a mistake.

NORMAN (*He stops at the bottom of the stairs*) I've only made two mistakes in my life. One was trusting you as my friend—the other was going out for the muscatel.
(*He continues up the stairs*)

ANDY   Norman, I've known you for eight years. Can you ever remember me lying to you *once* in all those eight years?

NORMAN   Yes. I've known you for nine years.
        (*He continues up the stairs*)

ANDY   All right, *nine* years. I don't care what you saw yesterday, I'm telling you the truth. I cannot abide that girl and she finds me snide, smug, and repulsive.

NORMAN (*Stops*)   I see. And I walked in just as she was sinking her fangs into your throat, and you fought off the attack with your mouth.

ANDY (*He goes up center*)   No, she was kissing me.

NORMAN   Kissing *you* . . . ? You're a foot taller than she is and you can't stand her. So the way I see it, the only way she could have kissed you against your wishes is for her to have nineteen-inch lips—and I just don't buy that.

ANDY   I don't care what you're buying, I did not make an overt act toward her.

NORMAN   In other words, she was the one who did the overting.

ANDY   Correct.

NORMAN   Why?

ANDY   Well—that's beside the point.

NORMAN   I think not. Why did she overt you right on the mouth?

ANDY   You're gonna laugh.

NORMAN   Try me.

ANDY   She likes the way I smell.

NORMAN (*He looks at his watch*)   It is now three o'clock. I will be hysterical until three-fifteen.
(*He continues up the stairs into the room*)

ANDY   What's so insane about it? *You* like the way *she* smells.

NORMAN (*He storms out*)   How can you even *mention* the two smells in the same breath?
(*He exits to his room*)

ANDY   Norman . . . (*He takes off his raincoat and tosses it on a high stool up left between the table and stairs*) You mean to tell me that after nine years of a personal, meaningful relationship, you would let that flag-waving sea urchin come between us?

NORMAN (*He comes out of his room and goes down the stairs to the landing*)   I can live with a slob, a sadist, a forger, or a junkie. I draw the line at finks.
(*He goes to the light-fixture on the landing and removes one bulb*)

ANDY (*He walks downstage to the desk*)   And what about the magazine?

96

NORMAN (*He comes down the stairs to the suitcase*)   The magazine is no longer my concern.
>   (*He puts the bulb in his suitcase and goes above the kitchen bar for the eight-pack of empty Coke bottles—takes half the bottles and packs them in the suitcase*)

ANDY   You—hypocrite! You pretend to be devoted and dedicated to an ideal that we've literally starved for, and you can blithely toss it all aside because we're suddenly embroiled in a romantic triangle!

NORMAN (*He goes to* ANDY)   *Now* I know why this magazine never made a cent. *Now* I know why we were starving. You, me, the girl and the Marine are a quadrangle, not a triangle!! You can't add!
>   (*He goes to the suitcase*)

ANDY   And what do you think you're going to do once you leave here?

NORMAN   In exactly thirty minutes I have an interview for a job with the A-P.

ANDY   Working at the checkout counter?

NORMAN   Not the A *and* P, you idiot. The A-P! The Associated-Press.

ANDY   Doing what?

NORMAN   I'm a writer. They'll pay me for writing . . . Just as, I imagine, you'll make your living by *finking!*
>   (*He goes to the closet*)

ANDY (*He goes left to upstage of the pole table*) A writer? Without me to push you, prod you, and encourage you, you couldn't hold down a job writing Rhode Island license plates.

NORMAN (*He comes out of the closet carrying two jackets on wooden hangers and goes stage left to* ANDY) No . . . ? LJ Seven-one-nine-six . . . ! And there's plenty more ideas where that came from.
    (*He gives the jackets to* ANDY *and takes the coat hangers to the duffle bag*)

ANDY All right, so we don't get along. Gilbert and Sullivan didn't speak to each other for fourteen years and they wrote twenty-three operettas together. Why can't we?

NORMAN (*At the sofa*) Gilbert never walked in and caught Sullivan kissing Poor Little Buttercup.

ANDY (*He puts the jackets on the up left table and then he goes right to the short wooden stool*) Okay, Norman, if I have to fight for my magazine, I'll fight for it.

NORMAN (*Looks at him in disbelief*) You're joking, surely.

ANDY Surely not.

NORMAN Andy, I'm warning you. I'm not wiry, but I'm thin. I'll cut you to ribbons.

ANDY I've already faced death with our paratrooper landlady. I'm not afraid of a skinny typist.
    (*He takes the short stool to the door. He sits on it and crosses his legs in a Gandhi fashion*)

NORMAN (*Looks at him*) What is that supposed to be?

ANDY What does it look like? It's a *sit-in!*

NORMAN (*He looks around to see if any sane person heard this lunatic remark. Then he moves up to the door*) If you don't get up from that sit-in, you're gonna see a *punch-down!*

ANDY Is that your answer to passive resistance?

NORMAN No, my answer to passive resistance is active kicking . . . Get up! What do you think you're doing?

ANDY The same as they did in Bombay in 1947 when twelve thousand Indians threw themselves across fifteen miles of railroad tracks.

NORMAN (*Looks at his watch, goes to his suitcase, closes it and picks it up. Then he goes to* ANDY) Well, Charley, in thirty seconds the five-fifteen is coming through.

ANDY (*Steeling himself*) Thou shalt not pass!

NORMAN Thou shalt bleed from both ears!

ANDY You would hit a man who wouldn't raise his arms in defense?

NORMAN Actually I prefer it that way.

ANDY Norman, if you go over to their side it's the end of free, creative thinking. They'll have you writing weather reports and shipping news.

99

NORMAN   In two minutes I bring in my first story about a dead man leaning against a door.

ANDY (*Looks at him, then gets up*)   All right, Norman . . . (*He returns the stool to right of radiator*) I had hoped to avoid bloodshed . . . (*He takes off his sweater*) But you leave me no recourse. The pain I am about to inflict is done purely on request.

NORMAN (*Looks at him in disbelief*)   Do you mean it is your intention to actually come to blows? Hard hitting and everything?

ANDY (*At the pole table, rolling up his shirt sleeves*)   My fist right on your deviated septum.

NORMAN   Knowing full well that on July sixteenth I finish a three-year course in Oriental combat?

ANDY   I intend to compensate by fighting dirty.

NORMAN (*He puts down his suitcase, takes off his jacket and puts it on the landing*)   Okay, Andy, as long as you know the score. I've been waiting six months to try this in a real-life situation. I had hoped my first victim would be a mugger, but you'll do nicely. (*Goes to the center table as he rolls up his shirt sleeves*) Oh, by the way. It's my legal obligation to warn you that karate may be hazardous to one's health.

ANDY   And let me warn you that I have never once in my life struck another human being in anger. (*Both ANDY and NORMAN pick up the center coffee table and carry it stage right*) I don't want to kill you, but I have no idea how strong I am. (*Goes left and takes the director's chair to the right of the desk*) If you feel yourself dying, just speak up.

> (NORMAN *tries to lift the right chair with one hand.* ANDY *comes to his rescue.* NORMAN *then carries the chair up right and puts it down near the table—he bows to the chair*)

NORMAN   Anytime you're ready.

ANDY   I'm ready if you are.

> (NORMAN *assumes a sort of professional pose while* ANDY *just tries to look menacing*)

NORMAN (*Smirks*)   Is that the way you're going to stand? You don't know the first thing you're doing. You won't last ten seconds.

ANDY   When you're able to talk again, you can teach me.

NORMAN   Can I show you the four basic positions? I'm still going to break your neck, but at least you'll look better. (*He goes toward* ANDY, *who growls at him*) This is ridiculous. You have no defense at all. I'm not even enjoying this.

> (*He goes stage right*)

ANDY   If you want entertainment, turn on the television. If you want to fight, come over here.

NORMAN   I want to fight . . .

> (*In true karate fashion,* NORMAN *takes a step towards* ANDY, *swipes at the air twice and grunts audi-*

bly in Japanese fashion. He repeats the move with the other hand and the sound)

ANDY   If you're gonna do that, why don't you put on those big white bloomers like the Japanese wear?

NORMAN   You must be out of your mind. (*Holds up his poised right hand*) Don't you realize this is a lethal weapon? This hand is trained to kill. Once I start it in motion, it can't be stopped. It's been trained that way. All right, Andy, I'm through toying with you. I'm gonna give you one chop (*Looks at his watch*) . . . and then I've got to go. (NORMAN *approaches* ANDY. *He raises his hand.* ANDY *runs upstage of the pole table and goes right.* NORMAN *follows him*) Damnit, Andy, why don't you stand still and fight like a man?

ANDY   Because I'm afraid, that's why.

NORMAN   I told you that before we started.

ANDY   Not of you, of myself. I am so seething, so fed up with your monumental stupidity and infantile behavior, that if I get within two inches of you, I swear by everything I believe in this world, I'll crack your head wide open.

NORMAN   Then you'd better do it to me before I do it to you.

ANDY   All right, damnit, here!! (*And in a karate-type swipe,* ANDY *swings at* NORMAN, *who simultaneously swings at him with an identical blow, but they succeed in landing both blows on each other's arms between the wrist and elbow, causing enormous pain to both. They both stop and rub their painful arms and moan together)* Oohhhh . . . Oh, boy, that hurts . . .

NORMAN *(Grimaces)* Oh, God, my arm, my arm.

ANDY *(Goes toward him)* Are you all right?

NORMAN *(Goes away to the pole table)* Let me alone. Why don't you look where you're hitting? In karate you hit the neck or the kidneys, not the arm. *(He looks at his wrist)* Ah, damn.

ANDY What's wrong?

NORMAN You broke my Benrus watch.

ANDY *(He takes a few steps left)* Let me see.

NORMAN It's broken. It's broken. There's nothing to see— it's my good watch, too.

ANDY I'm sorry.

NORMAN And I just put in a new crystal, and I had it cleaned.

ANDY Why didn't you take the watch off first?

NORMAN Because I didn't expect to get hit on the wrist. I told you you didn't know what you were doing . . . I don't want to fight anymore.
    (He goes right, downstage of ANDY*)*

ANDY Well, what are we gonna do?

NORMAN (*Putting on his jacket*) You can do whatever you want, I'm going.

ANDY For good?

NORMAN For good. I really don't like you anymore.

ANDY (*Turns away*) Okay, Norman, if you wanna go, then go. I think you're wrong, but if that's what you want (*Goes left to the desk*) I wish you the very best of luck.

NORMAN (*Looking at his watch again*) Boy, I really loved this watch, too.

ANDY (*He goes upstage of the pole table.* NORMAN *goes to his suitcase*) So, this is the end of *Fallout* magazine—you've got to admit it, Norm, for a while we had a good thing going here.

NORMAN (*Points to his watch*) If I knew what time it was, I'd hang around another ten minutes and watch you cry.

ANDY You don't think I'm sincere about our friendship.

NORMAN (*Picks up his suitcase*) For this magazine you would sell your own mother—who, incidentally, no one has seen for three years.

ANDY Norman, please believe me when I say I'd rather have a handshake from you right now—than the Pulitzer Prize. (*He extends his hand out to* NORMAN. NORMAN *looks at him, puts down his suitcase and goes left to* ANDY) What's the matter?

NORMAN   I'm afraid you're going to grab me and handcuff me to the steampipe.

ANDY (*He extends his hand again*)   Good-bye, Norman.

NORMAN   Good-bye, Andy. (NORMAN *extends his hand to* ANDY, *who in a flash of dexterity pulls up a pair of handcuffs from the pole table. One handcuff has been affixed to the steampipe, the other one* ANDY *puts on* NORMAN's *wrist. The handcuffs had been hidden by a pile of magazines. It happened so fast* NORMAN *is dumbfounded and can only stare blankly at what* ANDY *has done.* ANDY *rushes to remove the telephone from the pole table, puts it on the floor. He replaces the director's chair left center, pulls back the round center table and resets the chair right of the table*) You dirty, no-good rat, I even have to write your lousy ideas!
   (*He pulls on the handcuffs*)

ANDY   That one was my own, sweetheart. I heard you on the phone this morning with the A-P. Now we have one article to finish, one more page. And we're down to the finish line, Norman, because in forty-five minutes, Mr. Franklyn's two Neanderthal sons will be here to pick up our completed magazine or their six hundred dollars. And if I can't give them either one, I'll give them you.

NORMAN (*Looks at him in disbelief*)   You mean you're serious? You actually intend, in real life, to keep a human being chained to a steampipe?

ANDY (*He gets the typewriter from the sofa and takes it to the pole table*)   Until tomorrow—when the police find an unidentified broken object dangling from a post.
(*He puts the typewriter on the table*)

NORMAN   All right, Andy, I'm in no mood for the "Prisoner of Zenda." Open up!

ANDY   Not until I see some paper work.
(*He starts for the kitchen*)

NORMAN   Where are you going?

ANDY   To the kitchen to get myself a tiny-kumquat sandwich.
(*He goes into the kitchen*)

NORMAN (*Shouts toward the window*)   Help! Help! I'm being held prisoner! (*He looks out the window and shouts to someone*) Hey, lady! You wanna make a dollar? (*We hear a thunderous crash in the kitchen and a loud scream from ANDY*) What happened?
(*From the kitchen, ANDY staggers out holding his back in pain. He leans on the bar for support*)

ANDY   Why did you wax the kitchen floor?

NORMAN   Are you crazy? I didn't wax the kitchen floor.

ANDY (*Going toward a chair*)   Well, the kitchen floor is waxed and if you didn't wax it, who did?
(*The front door opens and SOPHIE enters carrying a package in tin foil in one hand and a red suitcase in the other*)

SOPHIE (*Leaving the suitcase at the door*) Ah've come to say good-bye. Ah froze a dozen fritters for you and be careful in the kitchen, Ah just waxed the floor.
(*She puts the fritters on the kitchen bar*)

NORMAN Sophie, he's gone crazy. Look what he's done to me. He's chained me to a steampipe!
(ANDY *sits in the chair*)

SOPHIE That won't be necessary anymore, Mr. Hobart. My bus is leavin' for Hunnicut in fifteen minutes. Since Ah only put in a three-day week Ah believe you have some money comin' back to you.
(*She pours the pennies out of her purse onto the center table and starts out*)

NORMAN Sophie, you don't have to leave because of me. I'm not going to bother you anymore. I didn't even smell you coming in here.

SOPHIE Ah'm glad, Norman. Ah'm not leavin' because of you. Ah don't blame you for the crazy way you been actin' lately. Ah understand it now. There are some things in life we just can't control. For no reason at all somethin' strange and mystifyin' hits us and there's nothin' anybody can do about it except just sit and wait and hope it goes away just as fast as it came. Unfortunately Ah don't see mine goin' away in the foreseeable future and that's why Ah decided Ah can't marry Lieutenant Burt Fenneman and that's why Ah'm gettin' on the bus to Hunnicut an' Ah can't say another word or else Ah'll start cryin' all over this room.
(*She starts to cry and runs toward the door, picking up her suitcase*)

ANDY Miss Rauschmeyer . . . Wait! (*She stops at the door and waits*) I am in great physical pain. I have a dislocated back from an overwaxed floor and a limp arm from a misguided karate chop. (*He rises from the chair*) But I just wanted you to know that I'm sorry—sorry that some of us react to certain stimuli, and that others of us don't. However, I have no wish to cause you any embarrassment or discomfort. Starting tomorrow I may be running this magazine myself. If you like, you can stay on— at half salary.

SOPHIE (*Puts her suitcase down outside the door and returns to the room*) You expect me to stay here with me feelin' the way Ah feel and you feelin' the way you don't . . . ? Mr. Hobart, if Ah wasn't afraid Ah'd miss mah bus, Ah'd really tell you somethin'. (*To* NORMAN) Do you have the time?

NORMAN (*Looks at his watch*) I don't even have a crystal.

SOPHIE (*To* ANDY) Well, Ah'll tell you anyway. You're right. Ah may be provincial and old-fashioned. Ah may believe in a lot of things like patriotism and the Constitution because that's the way Ah was brought up, and that's the way Ah feel. The trouble with you is you can't feel. You can't feel, you can't see, you can't hear and oh, boy, *you can't smell*. All you can do is think. But until you learn to use all those wonderful gadgets that nature has given you, you are only one-fifth of a man. Unfortunately by the time you get them all workin' and realize you are crazy about me, Ah will be back home in mah high school gymnasium gettin' in shape for next year's Olympics. If you want mah advice, Ah suggest you take those pennies and visit an eye, ear, nose and throat man.

(*Starts for the door*) And maybe you ought to see a dentist too. Because mah former fiancé, not happy with the recent turn of events, is on his way over here to separate your teeth from your face.

NORMAN (*Jumps up and down happily*) Now you're gonna get it! *Now* you'll first get it!
    (ANDY *sits*)

SOPHIE Did you hear what Ah said? There's an eight-foot Marine on his way here to chomp you up!

NORMAN (*Gleefully*) You hear that? The Yanks are coming! It's all over now, brother. (*Yells out the window*) Come on, Leathernecks. (*He sings the "Marine Hymn"*) I'm glad I'm chained to a pipe because I wouldn't miss this for anything.

SOPHIE (*With a big smile*) Ah wish Ah could stay to see it.

ANDY But you can't because you're leaving.

SOPHIE (*Goes to stairs leading to the front door*) That's right, Ah'm leavin'! Ah'm leavin'! Back to Hunnicut. And startin' tomorrow Ah'm gonna swim a mile every day from now until next summer. (*She comes down the steps and walks toward the center table*) Every American has to do what he does best for his country, and Ah can swim! Ah'm gonna swim the United States right into a gold medal and this time Ah'm gonna beat the livin' nose plugs offa that little fat girl from the desert. (*She picks the phone off the floor*) Ah'm usin' your phone one more time. (*She dials*) Gimme Western Union! (*To*

ANDY) And what you did to blacken America's good name with your protestin' magazine, Ah will whitewash with mah backstroke down in Mexico City. (*Into the phone*) Ah'd like to send a telegram, please. To Mr. Andrew Hobart, 217 Chestnut Hill, San Francisco. (*She looks at* ANDY) "Dear Mr. Hobart . . . Whether you like it or not, Ah pledge allegiance to the flag of the United States of America . . . And to the republic for which it stands, one nation, under God, indivisible, with liberty and justice for all." Sign that "A Patriot," and send it collect.

(*She hangs up, puts the phone back on the floor and exits with a flourish*)

NORMAN   You mean you're just going to sit there? She's going back to Hunnicut and you may never see her again!

ANDY   I'll see her again.

NORMAN   When?

ANDY   In 1972. I guarantee you she's the next President of the United States . . . Norman, I've had just about enough of you. Every man has his breaking point and my point just broke.

NORMAN   What are you gonna do?

ANDY   Murder! I'm going to commit cold-blooded murder right in this room. (*He rises and goes stage left*) I'm going to kill the only thing in this world that really means anything to me—my magazine. (*He takes the key and unlocks* NORMAN's *handcuffs*) There! Go on, you're free. Now get out of here and let me bury the body. (*He goes

to the bulletin board while NORMAN *goes center.* ANDY
rips down the credo sign and breaks it over his knee)
Maybe you were right. Maybe you were both right.
Maybe I am crazy. Maybe it was lunatic to try to hold on
to one tiny, not very important, insignificant little voice-
in-the-wilderness against such overwhelming odds as a
girl-smelling mental case and a wetback Martha Wash-
ington. (*He picks up the magazines from the pole table
and takes them right to the duffle bag on the sofa. Then
he puts the magazines into the bag)* I'm sure she'll be
very happy now. America is safe tonight. In tribute, tomorrow Howard Johnson's will add another flavor. (*He
throws the duffle bag on the floor)* She's won, don't you
see that, she's won. Divide and conquer, that's the way
they do it. Well, we're divided and we're conquered. The
war is over and we've surrendered. In reparations, she
gets the Polish corridor, the free city of Danzig, three
outfielders, two turtledoves and a partridge in a pear tree.
(*He collapses into the chair right of the table)*

NORMAN   Well—we can't always have what we want.

ANDY   Go on, you were in such a hurry to go, why don't
you go?

NORMAN (*Goes to the suitcase)*   Yeah . . . Want me to
help you straighten up before I go?

ANDY   I wouldn't want you to be late for your appoint-
ment.

NORMAN (*He nods and picks up the suitcase)*   One thing
you were right about. Physical attraction isn't enough.

It's like chewing gum. It starts off great, but the flavor doesn't last long.

ANDY   That's why they put five sticks in a pack. I'll see you, Norman.
(*He rises and goes up the steps to the landing*)

NORMAN   Any idea what you're gonna do now?

ANDY   I might go back to Philadelphia. Maybe work for my father.

NORMAN   I can't picture you in your father's business.

ANDY   I don't know. There's a lot of important work being done in the kitchen-cabinet field today.

NORMAN   Yeah. They say Formica is the hope of the future. (*He pauses*) I just want to say that if you decide not to go back to Philadelphia, that maybe someday, I don't know when, I'll be able to forget our differences, forget what's happened here the last few days, forget everything . . . And when I do, maybe someday I'll be back.

ANDY   I hope so, Norman . . . So long.
(NORMAN *nods and leaves. There is a moment's silence, then the door opens and* NORMAN *returns*)

NORMAN   I forgot everything; I'm back.

ANDY   What took you so long?

NORMAN (*He puts his suitcase down near the kitchen bar*)

I got stuck in traffic. (ANDY *comes down steps*) Hey, tell the truth! Were you really going back to Philadelphia?

ANDY Of course not. I was going to marry Mrs. Mackininee and open up the only discothèque funeral parlor in California.
(They break up laughing)

NORMAN And you'll be glad to know I'm Norman again. Norman the writer . . . (*He picks up the typewriter from the pole table*) Norman the man who's dedicated to this magazine.
(He goes upstage to the left window)

ANDY (*Closing the door*) And promise me you'll never go off the deep end over a girl like that again.

NORMAN (*At the window*) I'll promise tomorrow.

ANDY Why not today?

NORMAN 'Cause there's a gorgeous redhead across the street. (*Yells out*) Hey, beautiful redhead lady, I love you!

ANDY Norman, get back to that typewriter. (*He picks up the phone and puts it on the desk*) We've got a magazine to get out.

NORMAN (*Going to the desk. He sits*) All right. All right.

ANDY And promise me you won't get up from that chair until you finish.
(He picks up the dummy magazine from the desk)

113

NORMAN   My fingers are glued to the keys.

ANDY   No distractions?

NORMAN   No distractions.

ANDY (*Going stage right*)   No matter how much the smell in here is driving you crazy?

NORMAN   What smell?

ANDY   What do you mean, "what smell"? Her smell. Sophie.

NORMAN   I don't smell Sophie.

ANDY   Are you crazy? How can you not smell it? It's all over the room.

NORMAN   This room?

ANDY   Of course this room. She was just in here, wasn't she? I know the difference between a room-smell and a Sophie-smell and this is definitely—(*He drops the dummy magazine on the center table*) My God, what has happened to me?

NORMAN   You want me to chain you to the steampipe?

ANDY   It's not possible. These things don't happen to me. You were second in your class in Dartmouth, *but I was first*.

NORMAN   It's just physical attraction. That's not for us. It's for hippopotamuses.

ANDY (*Screaming*) I know that, damnit!

NORMAN What are you screaming for?

ANDY Because I'm standing here talking to you, and my hippopotamus is getting on the bus. (*Rushes right to the window on the landing*) Sophie! Sophie!
    (*The door flings open and* SOPHIE *rushes in but stops on the steps*)

SOPHIE Ah been standin' out there just prayin' you'd say mah name. If you didn't say it in two more minutes, Ah was gonna come back in here and say it for you.

ANDY (*Comes down the stairs*) You didn't get on the bus.

SOPHIE Ah didn't get on the bus because Ah'm not goin' anywhere. Ah heard everything you said and if you were gonna give up this subversive magazine Ah was personally gonna come in here and tear you apart mahself. (*Comes down one step*) Ah may not agree with what you say, but if you stop sayin' it, then no one will disagree and that is not the idea of democracy. (*Down one more step*) We got free speech in this country and Ah'm here to see that it stays free and spoken.

ANDY You really didn't get on the bus.

SOPHIE (*Goes right to* ANDY) Of course Ah didn't get on the bus. 'Cause in the first place Ah'm crazy about you and in the second place Ah left mah bus fare on your table.

ANDY If you had gone back to Hunnicut, I'd have done

something crazy like going after you on the next bus or the next train or the next plane or the next ship out of here.

(*The telephone rings.* NORMAN, *at the desk, picks it up*)

NORMAN (*Into the phone*) Thomas Cook Travel Agency . . . No, it's his friend, Norman.

SOPHIE Besides, Ah got a job here that pays me seventy-five dollars a week and Ah'm not about to give it up.

ANDY Seventy-*two* dollars. We've got to stick to the President's guide lines.

SOPHIE That's fine with me.

NORMAN (*On the phone*) That sounds wonderful. I'll be right there.
(*He hangs up and starts for the door*)

SOPHIE Where are you goin'?

NORMAN Skydiving with Mrs. Mackininee.

SOPHIE (*She takes a few steps to* NORMAN) You stay where you are and get back to work. We have a magazine to get out here. (*To* ANDY) Right?
(NORMAN *sits down again*)

ANDY Right! Only let me give you fair warning. It's not going to be easy. You start at eight and quit at seven.

SOPHIE That's fine with me!

ANDY   I want pencils sharpened and papers stacked.

SOPHIE That's fine with me!

ANDY   I want the books dusted, the floors cleaned and when I say hot coffee I mean hot coffee!

SOPHIE   That's fine with me!

ANDY   Good. Now that you know what the rules are . . . (*He goes to* NORMAN, *who is sitting at the desk*) Let's you and I get back to ripping apart the degenerating American way of life. Right?
(SOPHIE *follows*)

NORMAN   Right!

ANDY (*Turns to* SOPHIE)   And if you've got anything to say, say it to yourself . . . Okay! Now that we all understand each other, maybe we'll finally get a little work done around here.
(*Both* ANDY *and* SOPHIE *smell each other.* ANDY *crosses downstage of her, goes to the chair right of the center table and sits. He picks up the clipboard and goes to work.* NORMAN *starts typing.* SOPHIE *takes off her jacket and puts it on the back of the director's chair. She goes to the kitchen bar for the feather duster. As she starts dusting, she starts singing*)

SOPHIE (*She dusts the up left table and pole table*)
"Mine eyes have seen the glory of the coming of the Lord,

117

He is trampling out the vintage where the grapes of
wrath are stored,"

(*From the wings—no, from the heavens, we hear*
VOICES *joining* SOPHIE *in the stirring, building
strains of this, the most inspiring of all patriotic
hymns*)

"He hath loosed the fateful lightning of His terrible
swift sword:

His truth is marching on."

(*Curtain. The curtain goes back up immediately.*
SOPHIE *is busy dusting and singing. Both* ANDY *and*
NORMAN *look front incredulously. The curtain falls
—music rings out during the curtain calls*)

"Glory, glory, hallelujah!

Glory, glory, hallelujah!

Glory, glory, hallelujah!

His truth goes marching on."

Curtain

812
Si5s

STONEHAM PUBLIC LIBRARY

3 1509 00032 4700

LIBRARY

MASS.

812   Simon
Si5s   The star-spangled
        girl

PUBLIC LIBRARY
STONEHAM, MASS.